Ballads of Scottish T1 Romance Popular Ballads of the Olden Times - Third Series

Frank Sidgwick

Alpha Editions

This edition published in 2024

ISBN : 9789366385723

Design and Setting By
Alpha Editions
www.alphaedis.com
Email - info@alphaedis.com

As per information held with us this book is in Public Domain.
This book is a reproduction of an important historical work. Alpha Editions uses the best technology to reproduce historical work in the same manner it was first published to preserve its original nature. Any marks or number seen are left intentionally to preserve its true form.

PREFACE

ALTHOUGH a certain number of the ballads in this volume belong to England as much as to Scotland, the greater number are so intimately connected with Scottish history and tradition, that it would have been rash (to say the least) for a Southron to have ventured across the border unaided. It is therefore more than a pleasure to record my thanks to my friend Mr. A. Francis Steuart of Edinburgh, to whom I have submitted the proofs of these ballads. His extensive and peculiar knowledge of Scottish history and genealogy has been of the greatest service throughout.

I must also thank Mr. C. G. Tennant for assistance with the map given as frontispiece; and my unknown friend, Messrs. Constable's reader, has supplied valuable help in detail.

My self-imposed scheme of classification by subject-matter becomes no easier as the end of my task approaches. The Fourth Series will consist mainly of ballads of Robin Hood and other outlaws, including a few pirates. The projected class of 'Sea Ballads' has thus been split; *Sir Patrick Spence*, for example, appears in this volume. A few ballads defy classification, and will have to appear, if at all, in a miscellaneous section.

The labour of reducing to modern spelling several ballads from the seventeenth-century orthography of the Percy Folio is compensated, I hope, by the quaint and spirited result. These lively ballads are now presented for the first time in this popular form.

In *The Jolly Juggler*, given in the Appendix, I claim to have discovered a new ballad, which has not yet been treated as such, though I make bold to think Professor Child would have included it in his collection had he known of it. I trust that the publicity thus given to it will attract the attention of experts more competent than myself to annotate and illustrate it as it deserves.

F. S.

BALLADS IN THE THIRD SERIES

I HAVE hesitated to use the term 'historical' in choosing a general title for the ballads in this volume, although, if the word can be applied to any popular ballads, it would be applied with most justification to a large number of these ballads of Scottish and Border tradition. 'Some ballads are historical, or at least are founded on actual occurrences. In such cases, we have a manifest point of departure for our chronological investigation. The ballad is likely to have sprung up shortly after the event, and to represent the common rumo[u]r of the time. Accuracy is not to be expected, and indeed too great historical fidelity in detail is rather a ground of suspicion than a certificate of the genuinely popular character of the piece.... Two cautionary observations are necessary. Since history repeats itself, the possibility and even the probability must be entertained that every now and then a ballad which had been in circulation for some time was adapted to the circumstances of a recent occurrence, and has x come down to us only in such an adaptation. It is also far from improbable that many ballads which appear to have no definite localization or historical antecedents may be founded on fact, since one of the marked tendencies of popular narrative poetry is to alter or eliminate specific names of persons and places in the course of oral tradition.'[1]

Warned by these wise words, we may, perhaps, select the following ballads from the present volume as 'historical, or at least founded on actual occurrences.'

(i) This section, which we may call 'Historical,' includes *The Hunting of the Cheviot*, *The Battle of Otterburn*, *Mary Hamilton*, *The Laird o' Logie*, *Captain Car*, *Flodden Field*, *The Fire of Frendraught*, *Bessy Bell and Mary Gray*, *Jamie Douglas*, *Earl Bothwell*, *Durham Field*, *The Battle of Harlaw*, and *Lord Maxwell's Last Goodnight*. Probably we should add *The Death of Parcy Reed*; possibly *Geordie* and *The Gipsy Laddie*. More doubtful still is *Sir Patrick Spence*; and xi *The Baron of Brackley* confuses two historical events.

(ii) From the above section I have eliminated those which may be separately classified as 'Border Ballads.' *Sir Hugh in the Grime's Downfall* seems to have some historical foundation, but *Bewick and Grahame* has none. A sub-section of 'Armstrong Ballads' forms a good quartet; *Johnie Armstrong*, *Kinmont Willie*, *Dick o' the Cow*, and *John o' the Side*.

(iii) In the purely 'Romantic' class we may place *The Braes of Yarrow*, *The Twa Brothers*, *The Outlyer Bold*, *Clyde's Water*, *Katharine Jaffray*, *Lizie Lindsay*, *The Heir of Linne*, and *The Laird of Knottington*.

(iv) There remain a lyrical ballad, *The Gardener*; a song, *Waly, waly, gin love be bonny*; and the nondescript *Whummil Bore*. The Appendix contains a ballad, *The Jolly Juggler*, which would have come more fittingly in the First Series, had I known of it in time.

In the general arrangement, however, the above classes have been mixed, in order that the reader may browse as he pleases.

<u>1</u>. Introduction (p. xvi) to *English and Scottish Popular Ballads, edited from the Collection of Francis James Child*, by Helen Child Sargent and George Lyman Kittredge, 1905. This admirable condensation of Child's five volumes, issued since my Second Series, is enhanced by Professor Kittredge's *Introduction*, the best possible substitute for the gap left in the larger book by the death of Child before the completion of his task.

A comparison of the first two ballads in this volume will show the latitude with which it is xii possible for an historical incident to be treated by tradition. The Battle of Otterburn was fought in 1388; but our two versions belong to the middle of the sixteenth century. The English *Battle of Otterburn* is the more faithful to history, and refers (35.²) to 'the cronykle' as authority. *The Hunting of the Cheviot* was in the repertory of Richard Sheale (see First Series, *Introduction*, xxvii), who ends his version in the regular manner traditional amongst minstrels. Also, we have the broadside *Chevy Chase*, which well illustrates the degradation of a ballad in the hands of the hack-writers; this may be seen in many collections of ballads.

Mary Hamilton has a very curious literary history. If, *pendente lite*, we may assume the facts to be as suggested, pp. 44-46, it illustrates admirably Professor Kittredge's warning, quoted above, that ballads already in circulation may be adapted to the circumstances of a recent occurrence. But the incidents—betrayal, child-murder, and consequent execution—cannot have been uncommon in courts, at least in days of old; and it is quite probable that an early story was adapted, first to the incident of 1563, and again to the Russian story of 1718. Perhaps we may remark in passing that it is a pity that so repugnant a story should be attached to a ballad xiii containing such beautiful stanzas as the last four.

Captain Car is an English ballad almost contemporary with the Scottish incident which it records; and, from the fact of its including a popular burden, we may presume it was adapted to the tune. *Bessy Bell and Mary Gray*, which records a piece of Scottish news of no importance whatever, has become an English nursery rhyme. In *Jamie Douglas* an historical fact has been interwoven with a beautiful lyric. Indeed, the chances of corruption and contamination are infinite.

The long pathetic ballad of *Bewick and Grahame* is a link between the romantic ballads and the ballads of the Border, *Sir Hugh in the Grime's Downfall* connecting the Border ballads with the 'historical' ballads. The four splendid 'Armstrong ballads' also are mainly 'historical,' though *Dick o' the Cow* requires further elucidation. *Kinmont Willie* is under suspicion of being the work of Sir Walter Scott, who alone of all ballad-editors, perhaps, could have compiled a ballad good enough to deceive posterity. We cannot doubt the excellence of *Kinmont Willie*; but it would be tedious, as well as unprofitable, to collect the hundred details of manner, choice xiv of words, and expression, which discredit the authenticity of the ballad.

John o' the Side has not, I believe, been presented to readers in its present shape before. It is one of the few instances in which the English version of a ballad is better than the Scottish.

The Braes o' Yarrow is a good example of the Scottish lyrical ballad, the continued rhyme being very effective. *The Twa Brothers* has become a game, and *Lizie Lindsay* a song. *The Outlyer Bold* is a title I have been forced to give to a version of the ballad best known as *The Bonnie Banks o' Fordie*; this, it is true, might have come more aptly in the First Series. So also *Katharine Jaffray*, which enlarges the lesson taught in *The Cruel Brother* (First Series, p. 76), and adds one of its own.

The Heir of Linne is another of the naïve, delightful ballads from the Percy Folio, and in general style may be compared with *The Lord of Learne* in the Second Series (p. 182).

Little is to be said of *The Gardener* or *The Whummil Bore*, the former being almost a lyric, and the latter presumably a fragment. *Waly,* xv *waly*, is not a ballad at all, and is only included because it has become confused with *Jamie Douglas*.

The Jolly Juggler seems to be a discovery, and I commend it to the notice of those better qualified to deal with it. The curious fifth line added to each verse may be the work of some minstrel—a humorous addition to, or comment upon, the foregoing stanza. Certain Danish ballads exhibit this peculiarity, but I cannot find any Danish counterpart to the ballad in Prior's three volumes.

THE HUNTING OF THE CHEVIOT

THE TEXT here given is that of a MS. in the Bodleian Library (Ashmole 48) of about the latter half of the sixteenth century. It was printed by Hearne, and by Percy in the *Reliques*, and the whole MS. was edited by Thomas Wright for the Roxburghe Club in 1860. In this MS. *The Hunting of the Cheviot* is No. viii., and is subscribed 'Expliceth, quod Rychard Sheale.' Sheale is known to have been a minstrel of Tamworth, and it would appear that much of this MS. (including certain poems, no doubt his own) is in his handwriting—probably the book belonged to him. But the supposition that he was author of the *Hunting of the Cheviot*, Child dismisses as 'preposterous in the extreme.'

The other version, far better known as *Chevy Chase*, is that of the Percy Folio, published in the *Reliques*, and among the Pepys, Douce, Roxburghe, and Bagford collections of ballads. For the sake of differentiation this may be called the broadside form of the ballad, as it forms a striking example of the impairment of a traditional ballad when re-written for the broadside press. Doubtless it is the one known and commented on by Addison in his famous papers (Nos. 70 and 74) in the *Spectator* (1711), but it is not the one referred to by Sir Philip Sidney in his *Apologie*. Professor Child doubts if Sidney's ballad, 'being so evill apparelled in the dust and cobwebbes of that uncivill age,' is the traditional one here printed, which is 2 scarcely the product of an uncivil age; more probably Sidney had heard it in a rough and ancient form, 'sung,' as he says, 'but by some blind crouder, with no rougher voyce than rude stile.' 'The Hunttis of the Chevet' is mentioned as one of the 'sangis of natural music of the antiquite' sung by the shepherds in *The Complaynt of Scotland*, a book assigned to 1549.

THE STORY.—The *Hunting of the Cheviot* is a later version of the *Battle of Otterburn*, and a less conscientious account thereof. Attempts have been made to identify the *Hunting* with the Battle of Piperden (or Pepperden) fought in 1436 between a Percy and a Douglas. But the present ballad is rather an unauthenticated account of an historical event, which made a great impression on the public mind. Of that, its unfailing popularity on both sides of the Border, its constant appearance in broadside form, and its inclusion in every ballad-book, give the best witness.

The notable deed of Witherington (stanza 54) has many parallels. All will remember the warrior who

> '... when his legs were smitten off
>
> He fought upon his stumps.'

Tradition tells an identical story of 'fair maiden Lilliard' at the Battle of Ancrum Muir in 1545. Seneca mentions the feat. It occurs in the Percy Folio, Sir Graysteel (in *Eger and Grine*) fighting on one leg. Johnie Armstrong and Sir Andrew Barton both retire to 'bleed awhile' after being transfixed through the body. Finally, in an early saga, King Starkathr (Starkad) fights on after his head is cut off.

THE HUNTING OF THE CHEVIOT

1.

1.[5] 'magger' = maugre; *i.e.* in spite of.

THE Persë owt off Northombarlonde,

and avowe to God mayd he

That he wold hunte in the mowntayns

off Chyviat within days thre,

In the magger of doughtë Dogles,

and all that ever with him be.

2.

2.[4] 'let,' hinder.

The fattiste hartes in all Cheviat

he sayd he wold kyll, and cary them away:

'Be my feth,' sayd the dougheti Doglas agayn,

'I wyll let that hontyng yf that I may.'

3.

3.[2] 'meany,' band, company.

3.[4] 'the' = they; so constantly, 'shyars thre'; the districts (still called shires) of Holy Island, Norham, and Bamborough.

Then the Persë owt off Banborowe cam,

with him a myghtee meany,

With fifteen hondrith archares bold off blood and bone;

the wear chosen owt of shyars thre.

4.

This begane on a Monday at morn,

in Cheviat the hillys so he;

The chylde may rue that ys vn-born,

it wos the mor pittë.

5.

5.³ 'byckarte,' *i.e.* bickered, attacked the deer.

The dryvars thorowe the woodës went,

for to reas the dear;

Bomen byckarte vppone the bent

with ther browd aros cleare.

6.

6.¹ 'wyld,' deer.

6.³ *i.e.* through the groves darted.

Then the wyld thorowe the woodës went,

on every sydë shear;

Greahondës thorowe the grevis glent,

for to kyll thear dear.

7.

7.³ 'oware,' hour.

This begane in Chyviat the hyls abone,

yerly on a Monnyn-day;

Be that it drewe to the oware off none,

a hondrith fat hartës ded ther lay.

8.

8.¹ 'mort,' note of the bugle.

8.⁴ 'bryttlynge,' cutting up.

The blewe a mort vppone the bent,

the semblyde on sydis shear;

To the quyrry then the Persë went,

to se the bryttlynge off the deare.

9.

He sayd, 'It was the Duglas promys
this day to met me hear;
But I wyste he wolde faylle, verament;'
a great oth the Persë swear.

10.

10.² shaded his eyes with his hand.
At the laste a squyar off Northomberlonde
lokyde at his hand full ny;
He was war a the doughetie Doglas commynge,
with him a myghttë meany.

11.

Both with spear, bylle, and brande,
yt was a myghtti sight to se;
Hardyar men, both off hart nor hande,
wear not in Cristiantë.

12.

12.² 'feale,' fail.
12.⁴ 'yth,' in the.
The wear twenti hondrith spear-men good,
withoute any feale;
The wear borne along be the watter a Twyde,
yth bowndës of Tividale.

13.

13.² 'boÿs,' bows.
'Leave of the brytlyng of the dear,' he sayd,
'and to your boÿs lock ye tayk good hede;
For never sithe ye wear on your mothars borne
had ye never so mickle nede.'

14.

14.[3] 'glede,' glowing coal.

The dougheti Dogglas on a stede,

he rode alle his men beforne;

His armor glytteryde as dyd a glede;

a boldar barne was never born.

15.

'Tell me whos men ye ar,' he says,

'or whos men that ye be:

Who gave youe leave to hunte in this Chyviat chays,

in the spyt of myn and of me.'

16.

The first mane that ever him an answear mayd,

yt was the good lord Persë:

'We wyll not tell the whoys men we ar,' he says,

'nor whos men that we be;

But we wyll hounte hear in this chays,

in the spyt of thyne and of the.

17.

17.[4] 'the ton,' one or other.

'The fattiste hartës in all Chyviat

we have kyld, and cast to carry them away:'

'Be my troth,' sayd the doughetë Dogglas agayn,

'therfor the ton of us shall de this day.'

18.

Then sayd the doughtë Doglas

unto the lord Persë:

'To kyll alle thes giltles men,

alas, it wear great pittë!

19.

'But, Persë, thowe art a lord of lande,

I am a yerle callyd within my contrë;

Let all our men vppone a parti stande,

and do the battell off the and of me.'

20.

20.¹ 'cors,' curse.

'Nowe Cristes cors on his crowne,' sayd the lord Persë,

'who-so-ever ther-to says nay!

Be my troth, doughttë Doglas,' he says,

'thow shalt never se that day.

21.

21.⁴ 'on,' one.

'Nethar in Ynglonde, Skottlonde, nar France,

nor for no man of a woman born,

But, and fortune be my chance,

I dar met him, on man for on.'

22.

Then bespayke a squyar off Northombarlonde,

Richard Wytharyngton was his nam:

'It shall never be told in Sothe-Ynglonde,' he says,

'to Kyng Herry the Fourth for sham.

23.

'I wat youe byn great lordës twaw,

I am a poor squyar of lande:

I wylle never se my captayne fyght on a fylde,

and stande my selffe and loocke on,

But whylle I may my weppone welde,

I wylle not fayle both hart and hande.'

24.

24.³ 'And,' If.

That day, that day, that dredfull day!

the first fit here I fynde;

And youe wyll here any mor a the hountyng a the Chyviat,

yet ys ther mor behynde.

.   .   .   .   .

25.

25.⁴ 'sloughe,' slew.

The Yngglyshe men hade ther bowys yebent,

ther hartes wer good yenoughe;

The first off arros that the shote off,

seven skore spear-men the sloughe.

26.

26.⁴ 'wouche,' evil.

Yet byddys the yerle Doglas vppon the bent,

a captayne good yenoughe,

And that was sene verament,

for he wrought hom both woo and wouche.

27.

The Dogglas partyd his ost in thre,

lyk a cheffe cheften off pryde;

With suar spears off myghttë tre,

the cum in on every syde:

28.

Thrughe our Yngglyshe archery

gave many a wounde fulle wyde;

Many a doughetë the garde to dy,

which ganyde them no pryde.

29.

29.⁴ 'basnites,' light helmets or skull-caps.

The Ynglyshe men let ther boÿs be,

and pulde owt brandes that wer brighte;

It was a hevy syght to se

bryght swordes on basnites lyght.

30.

30.¹ 'myneyeple,' = manople, a kind of long gauntlet.

30.³ 'freyke,' man. So 32.¹, 47.¹, etc.

Thorowe ryche male and myneyeple,

many sterne the strocke done streght;

Many a freyke that was fulle fre,

ther undar foot dyd lyght.

31.

31.⁴ 'myllan,' Milan steel. Cp. 'collayne,' *Battle of Otterburn*, 54.⁴

At last the Duglas and the Persë met,

lyk to captayns of myght and of mayne;

The swapte togethar tylle the both swat

with swordes that wear of fyn myllan.

32.

Thes worthë freckys for to fyght,

ther-to the wear fulle fayne,

Tylle the bloode owte off thear basnetes sprente,

as ever dyd heal or rayn.

33.

'Yelde the, Persë,' sayde the Doglas,

'and i feth I shalle the brynge

Wher thowe shalte have a yerls wagis

of Jamy our Skottish kynge.

34.

'Thou shalte have thy ransom fre,

I hight the hear this thinge;

For the manfullyste man yet art thowe

that ever I conqueryd in filde fighttynge.'

35.

'Nay,' sayd the lord Persë,

'I tolde it the beforne,

That I wolde never yeldyde be

to no man of a woman born.'

36.

36.² 'wane.' One arrow out of a large number.—SKEAT.

With that ther cam an arrowe hastely,

forthe off a myghttë wane;

Hit hathe strekene the yerle Duglas

in at the brest-bane.

37.

Thorowe lyvar and longës bathe

the sharpe arrowe ys gane,

That never after in all his lyffe-days

he spayke mo wordës but ane:

That was, 'Fyghte ye, my myrry men, whyllys ye may,

for my lyff-days ben gan.'

38.

38.³ Addison compared (Vergil, *Aen.* x. 823):—
'Ingemuit miserans graviter dextramque tetendit,' etc.

The Persë leanyde on his brande,

and sawe the Duglas de;

He tooke the dede mane by the hande,

and sayd, 'Wo ys me for the!

39.

'To have savyde thy lyffe, I wolde have partyde with
my landes for years thre,
For a better man, of hart nare of hande,
was nat in all the north contrë.'

40.

Off all that se a Skottishe knyght,
was callyd Ser Hewe the Monggombyrry;
He sawe the Duglas to the deth was dyght,
he spendyd a spear, a trusti tre.

41.

41.³ 'blane,' lingered.

He rod uppone a corsiare
throughe a hondrith archery:
He never stynttyde, nar never blane,
tylle he cam to the good lord Persë.

42.

He set uppone the lorde Persë
a dynte that was full soare;
With a suar spear of a myghttë tre
clean thorow the body he the Persë ber,

43.

A the tothar syde that a man myght se
a large cloth-yard and mare:
Towe bettar captayns wear nat in Cristiantë
then that day slan wear ther.

44.

44.² 'say,' saw.

An archar off Northomberlonde

say slean was the lord Persë;

He bar a bende bowe in his hand,

was made off trusti tre.

45.

45.[2] *i.e.* till the point reached the wood of the bow.

An arow, that a cloth-yarde was lang,

to the harde stele halyde he;

A dynt that was both sad and soar

he sat on Ser Hewe the Monggombyrry.

46.

The dynt yt was both sad and sar,

that he of Monggomberry sete;

The swane-fethars that his arrowe bar

with his hart-blood the wear wete.

47.

47.[3] 'whylle the myghte dre' = while they might dree, as long as they could hold.

Ther was never a freake wone foot wolde fle,

but still in stour dyd stand,

Heawyng on yche othar, whylle the myghte dre,

with many a balfull brande.

48.

This battell begane in Chyviat

an owar befor the none.

And when even-songe bell was rang,

the battell was nat half done.

49.

The tocke ... on ethar hande

be the lyght off the mone;

Many hade no strenght for to stande,

- 15 -

in Chyviat the hillys abon.

50.

Of fifteen hondrith archars of Ynglonde

went away but seventi and thre;

Of twenti hondrith spear-men of Skotlonde,

but even five and fifti.

51.

But all wear slayne Cheviat within;

the hade no strengthe to stand on hy;

The chylde may rue that ys unborne,

it was the mor pittë.

52.

Thear was slayne, withe the lord Persë,

Sir Johan of Agerstone,

Ser Rogar, the hinde Hartly,

Ser Wyllyam, the bolde Hearone.

53.

53.[1] 'Loumle,' Lumley; previously printed Louele (= Lovel).

Ser Jorg, the worthë Loumle,

a knyghte of great renowen,

Ser Raff, the ryche Rugbe,

with dyntes wear beaten dowene.

54.

For Wetharryngton my harte was wo,

that ever he slayne shulde be;

For when both his leggis wear hewyne in to,

yet he knyled and fought on hys kny.

55.

Ther was slayne, with the dougheti Duglas,

Ser Hewe the Monggombyrry,

Ser Davy Lwdale, that worthë was,

his sistar's son was he.

56.

Ser Charls a Murrë in that place,

that never a foot wolde fle;

Ser Hewe Maxwelle, a lorde he was,

with the Doglas dyd he dey.

57.

57.[4] 'makys,' mates, husbands.

So on the morrowe the mayde them byears

off birch and hasell so gray;

Many wedous, with wepyng tears,

cam to fache ther makys away.

58.

58.[4] 'March-parti,' the Border; so 'the Marches,' 59.[3]

Tivydale may carpe off care,

Northombarlond may mayk great mon,

For towe such captayns as slayne wear thear

on the March-parti shall never be non.

59.

Word ys commen to Eddenburrowe,

to Jamy the Skottishe kynge,

That dougheti Duglas, lyff-tenant of the Marches,

he lay slean Chyviot within.

60.

60.[1] 'weal,' clench(?).

His handdës dyd he weal and wryng,

he sayd, 'Alas, and woe ys me!

- 17 -

Such an othar captayn Skotland within,'

he seyd, 'ye-feth shuld never be.'

61.

Worde ys commyn to lovly Londone,

till the fourth Harry our kynge,

That lord Persë, leyff-tenante of the Marchis,

he lay slayne Chyviat within.

62.

'God have merci on his solle,' sayde Kyng Harry,

'good lord, yf thy will it be!

I have a hondrith captayns in Ynglonde,' he sayd,

'as good as ever was he:

But, Persë, and I brook my lyffe,

thy deth well quyte shall be.'

63.

63.[4] The battle of Homildon Hill, near Wooler, Northumberland, was fought in 1402. See 1 *King Henry IV.*, Act I. sc. i.

As our noble kynge mayd his avowe,

lyke a noble prince of renowen,

For the deth of the lord Persë

he dyde the battell of Hombyll-down;

64.

Wher syx and thrittë Skottishe knyghtes

on a day wear beaten down:

Glendale glytteryde on ther armor bryght,

over castille, towar, and town.

65.

65.[2] 'spurn' = kick(?): Child suggests the reading:—'That ear [= e'er] began this spurn!' as a lament. But the whole meaning is doubtful.

- 18 -

This was the hontynge off the Cheviat,

that tear begane this spurn;

Old men that knowen the grownde well yenoughe

call it the battell of Otterburn.

66.

At Otterburn begane this spurne

uppone a Monnynday;

Ther was the doughtë Doglas slean,

the Persë never went away.

67.

67.[4] as the rain does.

Ther was never a tym on the Marche-partës

sen the Doglas and the Persë met,

But yt ys mervele and the rede blude ronne not,

as the reane doys in the stret.

68.

68.[1] 'our balys bete,' our misfortunes relieve.

Ihesue Crist our balys bete,

and to the blys vs brynge!

Thus was the hountynge of the Chivyat:

God send vs alle good endyng!

THE BATTLE OF OTTERBURN

THE TEXT is given mainly from the Cotton MS., Cleopatra C. iv. (*circa* 1550). It was printed by Percy in the fourth edition of the *Reliques*; in the first edition he gave it from Harleian MS. 293, which text also is made use of here. A separate Scottish ballad was popular at least as early as 1549, and arguments to prove that it was derived from the English ballad are as inconclusive as those which seek to prove the opposite.

THE STORY.—The battle of Otterburn was fought on Wednesday, August 19, 1388. The whole story is given elaborately by Froissart, in his usual lively style, but is far too long to be inserted here. It may, however, be condensed as follows.

The great northern families of Neville and Percy being at variance owing to the quarrels of Richard II. with his uncles, the Scots took the advantage of preparing a raid into England. Earl Percy, hearing of this, collected the Northumbrian powers; and, unable to withstand the force of the Scots, determined to make a counter-raid on the east or west of the border, according as the Scots should cross. The latter, hearing of the plan through a spy, foiled it by dividing their army into two parts, the main body under Archibald Douglas being directed to Carlisle. Three or four hundred picked men-at-arms, with two thousand archers and others, under James, Earl of Douglas, Earl of March and Dunbar, and the Earl of Murray, were to aim at Newcastle, and burn and ravage the bishopric of Durham. With the latter alone we are now concerned.

With his small army the Earl of Douglas passed rapidly through Northumberland, crossed the Tyne near Brancepeth, wasted the country as far as the gates of Durham, and returned to Newcastle as rapidly as they had advanced. Several skirmishes took place at the barriers of the town: and in one of these Sir Henry Percy (Hotspur) was personally opposed to Douglas. After an obstinate struggle the Earl won the pennon of the English leader, and boasted that he would carry it to Scotland, and set it high on his castle of Dalkeith. 'That,' cried Hotspur, 'no Douglas shall ever do, and ere you leave Northumberland you shall have small cause to boast.' 'Your pennon,' answered Douglas, 'shall this night be placed before my tent; come and win it if you can.' But the Scots were suffered to retreat without any hostile attempts on the part of the English, and accordingly, after destroying the tower of Ponteland, they came on the second day to the castle of Otterburn, situated in Redesdale, about thirty-two miles from Newcastle. The rest may be read in the ballad.

'Of all the battayles,' says Froissart, 'that I have made mention of here before, in all thys hystorye, great or small, thys battayle was one of the sorest, and best foughten, without cowards or faint hertes: for ther was nother knyght nor squyre but that dyde hys devoyre, and fought hand to hand.'

THE BATTLE OF OTTERBURN

1.

1.[3] 'bowynd,' hied.

YT fell abowght the Lamasse tyde,

Whan husbondes Wynnes ther haye,

The dowghtye Dowglasse bowynd hym to ryde,

In Ynglond to take a praye.

2.

2.[4] 'raysse,' raid.

The yerlle of Fyffe, wythowghten stryffe,

He bowynd hym over Sulway;

The grete wolde ever to-gether ryde;

That raysse they may rewe for aye.

3.

3. 'Hoppertope,' Ottercap (now Ottercaps) Hill, in the parish of Kirk Whelpington, Tynedale Ward, Northumberland. 'Rodclyffe crage' (now Rothby Crags), a cliff near Rodeley, south-east of Ottercap. 'Grene Lynton,' a corruption of Green Leyton, south-east of Rodely.—PERCY.

Over Hoppertope hyll they cam in,

And so down by Rodclyffe crage;

Vpon Grene Lynton they lyghted dowyn,

Styrande many a stage.

4.

And boldely brente Northomberlond,

And haryed many a towyn;

They dyd owr Ynglyssh men grete wrange,

To battell that were not bowyn.

5.

Than spake a berne vpon the bent,

Of comforte that was not colde,

And sayd, 'We have brente Northomberlond,

We have all welth in holde.

5.¹ 'berne,' man.

6.

'Now we have haryed all Bamborowe schyre,

All the welth in the world have wee;

I rede we ryde to Newe Castell,

So styll and stalworthlye.'

7.

Vpon the morowe, when it was day,

The standerds schone full bryght;

To the Newe Castell the toke the waye,

And thether they cam full ryght.

8.

8.¹ Sir Henry Percy (Hotspur), killed at Shrewsbury fifteen years after Otterburn.

8.³ 'march-man,' borderer. Percy is said to have been appointed Governor of Berwick and Warden of the Marches in 1385.

Syr Henry Perssy laye at the New Castell,

I tell yow wythowtten drede;

He had byn a march-man all hys dayes,

And kepte Barwyke upon Twede.

9.

To the Newe Castell when they cam,

The Skottes they cryde on hyght,

'Syr Hary Perssy, and thow byste within,

Com to the fylde, and fyght.

10.

'For we have brente Northomberlonde,

Thy erytage good and ryght,

And syne my logeyng I have take,

Wyth my brande dubbyd many a knyght.'

11.

Syr Harry Perssy cam to the walles,

The Skottyssch oste for to se,

And sayd, 'And thow hast brente Northomberlond,

Full sore it rewyth me.

12.

12.[4] 'The tone,' one or other.

'Yf thou hast haryed all Bamborowe schyre,

Thow hast done me grete envye;

For the trespasse thow hast me done,

The tone of vs schall dye.'

13.

'Where schall I byde the?' sayd the Dowglas,

'Or where wylte thow com to me?'

'At Otterborne, in the hygh way,

Ther mast thow well logeed be.

14.

14.[1] 'I have harde say that Chivet Hills stretchethe XX miles. Theare is greate plente of Redde Dere, and Roo Bukkes.'— *Leland's Itinerary.*

'The roo full rekeles ther sche rinnes,

To make the game and glee;

The fawken and the fesaunt both,

Amonge the holtes on hye.

15.

15.³ 'the tyll' = thee till, to thee.

'Ther mast thow haue thy welth at wyll,

Well looged ther mast be;

Yt schall not be long or I com the tyll,'

Sayd Syr Harry Perssye.

16.

'Ther schall I byde the,' sayd the Dowglas,

'By the fayth of my bodye':

'Thether schall I com,' sayd Syr Harry Perssy,

'My trowth I plyght to the.'

17.

A pype of wyne he gaue them over the walles,

For soth as I yow saye;

Ther he mayd the Dowglasse drynke,

And all hys ost that daye.

18.

The Dowglas turnyd hym homewarde agayne,

For soth withowghten naye;

He toke his logeyng at Oterborne,

Vpon a Wedynsday.

19.

19.¹ 'pyght,' fixed.

And ther he pyght hys standerd dowyn,

Hys gettyng more and lesse,

And syne he warned hys men to goo

To chose ther geldynges gresse.

20.

A Skottysshe knyght hoved vpon the bent,

A wache I dare well saye;

So was he ware on the noble Perssy

In the dawnyng of the daye.

21.

He prycked to hys pavyleon-dore,

As faste as he myght ronne;

'Awaken, Dowglas,' cryed the knyght,

'For hys love that syttes in trone.

22.

22.² 'wynne,' pleasure.

'Awaken, Dowglas,' cryed the knyght,

'For thow maste waken wyth wynne;

Yender haue I spyed the prowde Perssye,

And seven stondardes wyth hym.'

23.

'Nay by my trowth,' the Dowglas sayed,

'It ys but a fayned taylle;

He durst not loke on my brede banner

For all Ynglonde so haylle.

24.

24.⁴ *i.e.* he could not give me my fill (of defeat).

'Was I not yesterdaye at the Newe Castell,

That stondes so fayre on Tyne?

For all the men the Perssy had,

He coude not garre me ones to dyne.'

25.

25.² *i.e.* to see if it were false.

He stepped owt at his pavelyon-dore,

- 25 -

To loke and it were lesse:

'Araye yow, lordynges, one and all,

For here begynnes no peysse.

26.

26.1 'eme,' uncle.

26.3 'cawte,' wary.

'The yerle of Mentaye, thow arte my eme,

The fowarde I gyve to the:

The yerlle of Huntlay, cawte and kene,

He schall be wyth the.

27.

'The lorde of Bowghan, in armure bryght,

On the other hand he schall be;

Lord Jhonstoune and Lorde Maxwell,

They to schall be with me.

28.

'Swynton, fayre fylde vpon your pryde!

To batell make yow bowen

Syr Davy Skotte, Syr Water Stewarde,

Syr Jhon of Agurstone!'

29.

29.4 'hyght,' promised.

The Perssy cam byfore hys oste,

Wych was ever a gentyll knyght;

Vpon the Dowglas lowde can he crye,

'I wyll holde that I haue hyght.

30.

'For thou haste brente Northomberlonde,

And done me grete envye;

For thys trespasse thou hast me done,

The tone of vs schall dye.'

31.

The Dowglas answerde hym agayne,

Wyth grett wurdes vpon hye,

And sayd, 'I have twenty agaynst thy one,

Byholde, and thou maste see.'

32.

32.⁴ 'schoote,' dismissed.

Wyth that the Perssy was grevyd sore,

For soth as I yow saye:

He lyghted dowyn vpon his foote,

And schoote hys horsse clene awaye.

33.

33.² *i.e.* who was ever royal among the rout.

Every man sawe that he dyd soo,

That ryall was ever in rowght;

Every man schoote hys horsse hym froo,

And lyght hym rowynde abowght.

34.

Thus Syr Hary Perssye toke the fylde,

For soth as I yow saye;

Jhesu Cryste in hevyn on hyght

Dyd helpe hym well that daye.

35.

35.² 'layne,' lie; so 40.²

But nyne thowzand, ther was no moo,

The cronykle wyll not layne;

Forty thowsande of Skottes and fowre

That day fowght them agayne.

36.

But when the batell byganne to joyne,

In hast ther cam a knyght;

The letters fayre furth hath he tayne,

And thus he sayd full ryght:

37.

'My lorde your father he gretes yow well,

Wyth many a noble knyght;

He desyres yow to byde

That he may see thys fyght.

38.

'The Baron of Grastoke ys com out of the west,

With hym a noble companye;

All they loge at your fathers thys nyght,

And the batell fayne wolde they see.'

39.

'For Jhesus love,' sayd Syr Harye Perssy,

'That dyed for yow and me,

Wende to my lorde my father agayne,

And saye thow sawe me not wyth yee.

40.

'My trowth ys plyght to yonne Skottysh knyght,

It nedes me not to layne,

That I schalde byde hym upon thys bent,

And I have hys trowth agayne.

41.

41.[1] *i.e.* if I wend off this ground.

'And if that I weynde of thys growende,

For soth, onfowghten awaye,

He wolde me call but a kowarde knyght

In hys londe another daye.

42.

42.¹ *i.e.* I had rather be flayed.

'Yet had I lever to be rynde and rente,

By Mary, that mykkel maye,

Then ever my manhood schulde be reprovyd

Wyth a Skotte another daye.

43.

43.³ 'waryson,' reward.

'Wherefore schote, archars, for my sake,

And let scharpe arowes flee:

Mynstrell, playe up for your waryson,

And well quyt it schall bee.

44.

44.² 'marke hym,' commit himself (by signing the cross).

'Every man thynke on hys trewe-love,

And marke hym to the Trenite;

For to God I make myne avowe

Thys day wyll I not flee.'

45.

The blodye harte in the Dowglas armes,

Hys standerde stood on hye,

That every man myght full well knowe;

By syde stode starrës thre.

46.

The whyte lyon on the Ynglyssh perte,

For soth as I yow sayne,

The lucettes and the cressawntes both;

The Skottes faught them agayne.

47.

Vpon Sent Androwe lowde can they crye,

And thrysse they schowte on hyght,

And syne merked them one owr Ynglysshe men,

As I haue tolde yow ryght.

48.

Sent George the bryght, owr ladyes knyght,

To name they were full fayne:

Owr Ynglyssh men they cryde on hyght,

And thrysse the schowtte agayne.

49.

Wyth that scharpe arowes bygan to flee,

I tell yow in sertayne;

Men of armes byganne to joyne,

Many a dowghty man was ther slayne.

50.

50.4 'collayne,' of Cologne steel. Cp. 'myllan,' *Hunting of the Cheviot*, 31.4

The Perssy and the Dowglas mette,

That ether of other was fayne;

They swapped together whyll that the swette,

Wyth swordes of fyne collayne:

51.

51.2 'roke,' reek, vapour.

Tyll the bloode from ther bassonnettes ranne,

As the roke doth in the rayne;

'Yelde the to me,' sayd the Dowglas,

'Or elles thow schalt be slayne.

52.

'For I see by thy bryght bassonet,

Thow arte sum man of myght;

And so I do by thy burnysshed brande;

Thow arte an yerle, or elles a knyght.'

53.

'By my good faythe,' sayd the noble Perssye,

'Now haste thou rede full ryght;

Yet wyll I never yelde me to the,

Whyll I may stonde and fyght.'

54.

They swapped together whyll that they swette,

Wyth swordës scharpe and long;

Ych on other so faste thee beette,

Tyll ther helmes cam in peyses dowyn.

55.

55.[2] 'stounde,' moment of time, hour.

The Perssy was a man of strenghth,

I tell yow, in thys stounde;

He smote the Dowglas at the swordes length

That he fell to the growynde.

56.

The sworde was scharpe, and sore can byte,

I tell yow in sertayne;

To the harte he cowde hym smyte,

Thus was the Dowglas slayne.

57.

The stonderdes stode styll on eke a syde,

Wyth many a grevous grone;

Ther the fowght the day, and all the nyght,

And many a dowghty man was slayne.

58.

58.³ 'drye' = dree, endure.

Ther was no freke that ther wolde flye,

But styffely in stowre can stond,

Ychone hewyng on other whyll they myght drye,

Wyth many a bayllefull bronde.

59.

Ther was slayne vpon the Skottës syde,

For soth and sertenly,

Syr James a Dowglas ther was slayne,

That day that he cowde dye.

60.

60.² 'grysely,' frightfully, grievously.

The yerlle of Mentaye he was slayne,

Grysely groned upon the growynd;

Syr Davy Skotte, Syr Water Stewarde,

Syr Jhon of Agurstoune.

61.

Syr Charllës Morrey in that place,

That never a fote wold flee;

Syr Hewe Maxwell, a lord he was,

Wyth the Dowglas dyd he dye.

62.

Ther was slayne upon the Skottës syde,

For soth as I yow saye,

Of fowre and forty thowsande Scottes

Went but eyghtene awaye.

63.

Ther was slayne upon the Ynglysshe syde,

For soth and sertenlye,

A gentell knyght, Syr Jhon Fechewe,

Yt was the more pety.

64.

Syr James Hardbotell ther was slayne,

For hym ther hartes were sore;

The gentyll Lovell ther was slayne,

That the Perssys standerd bore.

65.

Ther was slayne upon the Ynglyssh perte,

For soth as I yow saye,

Of nyne thowsand Ynglyssh men

Fyve hondert cam awaye.

66.

The other were slayne in the fylde;

Cryste kepe ther sowlles from wo!

Seyng ther was so fewe fryndes

Agaynst so many a foo.

67.

67.[4] 'makes,' mates.

Then on the morne they mayde them beerys

Of byrch and haysell graye;

Many a wydowe, wyth wepyng teyres,

Ther makes they fette awaye.

68.

Thys fraye bygan at Otterborne,

Bytwene the nyght and the day;

Ther the Dowglas lost hys lyffe,
And the Perssy was lede awaye.

69.

69.4 'borowed,' ransomed, set free.

Then was ther a Scottysh prisoner tayne,
Syr Hewe Mongomery was hys name;
For soth as I yow saye,
He borowed the Perssy home agayne.

70.

Now let us all for the Perssy praye
To Jhesu most of myght,
To bryng hys sowlle to the blysse of heven,
For he was a gentyll knyght.

JOHNIE ARMSTRONG

THE TEXT is taken from *Wit Restor'd*, 1658, where it is called *A Northern Ballet*. From the same collection comes the version of *Little Musgrave and Lady Barnard* given in First Series, p. 19. The version popularly known as *Johnny Armstrong's Last Good-Night*, so dear to Goldsmith, and sung by the Vicar of Wakefield, is a broadside found in most of the well-known collections.

THE STORY of the ballad has the authority of more than one chronicle, and is attributed to the year 1530. James V., in spite of the promise 'to doe no wrong' in his large and long letter, appears to have been incensed at the splendour of 'Jonnë's' retinue. It seems curious that the outlaw should have been a Westmoreland man; but the *Cronicles of Scotland* say that 'from the Scots border to Newcastle of England, there was not one, of whatsoever estate, but paid to this John Armstrong a tribute, to be free of his cumber, he was so doubtit in England.' Jonnë's offer in the stanza 16.[3,4], may be compared to the similar feat of Sir Andrew Barton.

JOHNIE ARMSTRONG

1.

THERE dwelt a man in faire Westmerland,

Jonnë Armestrong men did him call,

He had nither lands nor rents coming in,

Yet he kept eight score men in his hall.

2.

He had horse and harness for them all,

Goodly steeds were all milke-white;

O the golden bands an about their necks,

And their weapons, they were all alike.

3.

Newes then was brought unto the king

That there was sicke a won as hee,

That livëd lyke a bold out-law,

And robbëd all the north country.

4.
The king he writt an a letter then,
A letter which was large and long;
He signëd it with his owne hand,
And he promised to doe him no wrong.
5.
When this letter came Jonnë untill,
His heart it was as blyth as birds on the tree:
'Never was I sent for before any king,
My father, my grandfather, nor none but mee.
6.
'And if wee goe the king before,
I would we went most orderly;
Every man of you shall have his scarlet cloak,
Laced with silver laces three.
7.
'Every won of you shall have his velvett coat,
Laced with sillver lace so white;
O the golden bands an about your necks,
Black hatts, white feathers, all alyke.'
8.
By the morrow morninge at ten of the clock,
Towards Edenburough gon was hee,
And with him all his eight score men;
Good lord, it was a goodly sight for to see!
9.
When Jonnë came befower the king,
He fell downe on his knee;
'O pardon, my soveraine leige,' he said,

'O pardon my eight score men and mee.'

10.

'Thou shalt have no pardon, thou traytor strong,

For thy eight score men nor thee;

For to-morrow morning by ten of the clock,

Both thou and them shall hang on the gallow-tree.'

11.

But Jonnë looked over his left shoulder,

Good Lord, what a grevious look looked hee!

Saying, 'Asking grace of a graceles face—

Why there is none for you nor me.'

12.

But Jonnë had a bright sword by his side,

And it was made of the mettle so free,

That had not the king stept his foot aside,

He had smitten his head from his faire boddë.

13.

Saying, 'Fight on, my merry men all,

And see that none of you be taine;

For rather than men shall say we were hange'd,

Let them report how we were slaine.'

14.

Then, God wott, faire Eddenburrough rose,

And so besett poore Jonnë rounde,

That fowerscore and tenn of Jonnë's best men

Lay gasping all upon the ground.

15.

Then like a mad man Jonnë laide about,

And like a mad man then fought hee,

Untill a falce Scot came Jonnë behinde,
And runn him through the faire boddee.
16.
Saying, 'Fight on, my merry men all,
And see that none of you be taine;
For I will stand by and bleed but awhile,
And then will I come and fight againe.'
17.
Newes then was brought to young Jonnë Armestrong
As he stood by his nurse's knee,
Who vowed if ere he live'd for to be a man,
O' the treacherous Scots reveng'd hee'd be.

THE BRAES OF YARROW

THE TEXT was communicated to Percy by Dr. Robertson of Edinburgh, but it did not appear in the *Reliques*.

In 9.1, 'Then' is doubtless an interpolation, as are the words 'Now Douglas' in 11.1 But on the whole it is the best text of the fifteen or twenty variants.

THE STORY.—James Hogg and Sir Walter Scott referred the ballad to two different sources, the former legendary, and the latter historical. It has always been very popular in Scotland, and besides the variants there are in existence several imitations, such as the well-known poem of William Hamilton, 'Busk ye, busk ye, my bonny bonny bride.' This was printed in vol. ii. of Percy's *Reliques*.

About half the known variants make the hero and heroine man and wife, the other half presenting them as unmarried lovers.

THE BRAES OF YARROW

1.

'I dreamed a dreary dream this night,

That fills my heart wi' sorrow;

I dreamed I was pouing the heather green

Upon the braes of Yarrow.

2.

'O true-luve mine, stay still and dine,

As ye ha' done before, O;'

'O I'll be hame by hours nine,

And frae the braes of Yarrow.'

3.

'I dreamed a dreary dream this night,

That fills my heart wi' sorrow;

I dreamed my luve came headless hame,

O frae the braes of Yarrow!

4.

'O true-luve mine, stay still and dine.
As ye ha' done before, O;'
'O I'll be hame by hours nine,
And frae the braes of Yarrow.'

5.

'O are ye going to hawke,' she says,
'As ye ha' done before, O?
Or are ye going to wield your brand,
Upon the braes of Yarrow?'

6.

'O I am not going to hawke,' he says,
'As I have done before, O,
But for to meet your brother John,
Upon the braes of Yarrow.'

7.

7.1 'dowy,' dreary.
7.3 'well-wight,' brave, sturdy.

As he gaed down yon dowy den,
Sorrow went him before, O;
Nine well-wight men lay waiting him,
Upon the braes of Yarrow.

8.

'I have your sister to my wife,
Ye think me an unmeet marrow!
But yet one foot will I never flee
Now frae the braes of Yarrow.'

9.

Then four he kill'd and five did wound,
That was an unmeet marrow!

And he had weel nigh wan the day

Upon the braes of Yarrow.

10.

But a cowardly loon came him behind,

Our Lady lend him sorrow!

And wi' a rappier pierced his heart,

And laid him low on Yarrow.

11.

Now Douglas to his sister's gane,

Wi' meikle dule and sorrow:

'Gae to your luve, sister,' he says,

'He's sleeping sound on Yarrow.'

12.

As she went down yon dowy den,

Sorrow went her before, O;

She saw her true-love lying slain

Upon the braes of Yarrow.

13.

13. Apparently Percy's invention.

She swoon'd thrice upon his breist

That was her dearest marrow;

Said, 'Ever alace, and wae the day

Thou went'st frae me to Yarrow!'

14.

14.[3] 'wiped': Child suggests the original word was 'drank.'

She kist his mouth, she kaimed his hair,

As she had done before, O;

She wiped the blood that trickled doun

Upon the braes of Yarrow.

15.

15.[2] 'side,' long.

15.[3] 'hause-bane,' neck.

Her hair it was three quarters lang,

It hang baith side and yellow;

She tied it round her white hause-bane,

And tint her life on Yarrow.

THE TWA BROTHERS

THE TEXT is from Sharpe's *Ballad Book* (1823). Scott included no version of this ballad in his *Minstrelsy*; but Motherwell and Jamieson both had traditional versions. Motherwell considered it essential that the deadly wound should be accidental; but it is far more typical of a ballad-hero that he should lose his temper and kill his brother; and, as Child points out, it adds to the pathetic generosity of the slain brother in providing excuses for his absence to be made to his father, mother, and sister.

THE STORY.—Motherwell and Sharpe were more or less convinced that the ballad was founded on an accident that happened in 1589 to a Somerville, who was killed by his brother's pistol going off.

This ballad is still in circulation in the form of a game amongst American children—the last state of more than one old ballad otherwise extinct.

THE TWA BROTHERS

1.

1.4 'warsle,' wrestle.

THERE were twa brethren in the north,
They went to the school thegither;
The one unto the other said,
'Will you try a warsle afore?'

2.

They warsled up, they warsled down,
Till Sir John fell to the ground,
And there was a knife in Sir Willie's pouch,
Gied him a deadlie wound.

3.

'Oh brither dear, take me on your back,
Carry me to yon burn clear,
And wash the blood from off my wound,
And it will bleed nae mair.'

4.

He took him up upon his back,

Carried him to yon burn clear,

And washd the blood from off his wound,

But aye it bled the mair.

5.

'Oh brither dear, take me on your back,

Carry me to yon kirk-yard,

And dig a grave baith wide and deep,

And lay my body there.'

6.

He's taen him up upon his back,

Carried him to yon kirk-yard,

And dug a grave baith deep and wide,

And laid his body there.

7.

'But what will I say to my father dear,

Gin he chance to say, Willie, whar's John?'

'Oh say that he's to England gone,

To buy him a cask of wine.'

8.

'And what will I say to my mother dear,

Gin she chance to say, Willie, whar's John?'

'Oh say that he's to England gone,

To buy her a new silk gown.'

9.

'And what will I say to my sister dear,

Gin she chance to say, Willie, whar's John?'

'Oh say that he's to England gone,

To buy her a wedding ring.'

10.

'But what will I say to her you lo'e dear,

Gin she cry, Why tarries my John?'

'Oh tell her I lie in Kirk-land fair,

And home again will never come.'

THE OUTLYER BOLD

THE TEXT is taken from Motherwell's MS., which contains two versions; Motherwell printed a third in his *Minstrelsy,—Babylon; or, The Bonnie Banks o' Fordie*. Kinloch called the ballad the *Duke of Perth's Three Daughters*. As the following text has no title, I have ventured to give it one. 'Outlyer' is, of course, simply 'a banished man.'

THE STORY is much more familiar in all the branches of the Scandinavian race than in England or Scotland. In Denmark it appears as *Herr Truels' Daughters* or *Herr Thor's Children*; in Sweden as *Herr Torës' Daughters*. Iceland and Faroe give the name as Torkild or Thorkell.

The incidents related in this ballad took place (i) in Scotland on the bonnie banks o' Fordie, near Dunkeld; (ii) in Sweden in five or six different places; and (iii) in eight different localities in Denmark.

THE OUTLYER BOLD

> 1.
>
> THERE were three sisters, they lived in a bower,
>
> *Sing Anna, sing Margaret, sing Marjorie*
>
> The youngest o' them was the fairest flower.
>
> *And the dew goes thro' the wood, gay ladie*
>
> 2.
>
> The oldest of them she's to the wood gane,
>
> To seek a braw leaf and to bring it hame.
>
> 3.
>
> There she met with an outlyer bold,
>
> Lies many long nights in the woods so cold.
>
> 4.
>
> 4.[1] 'Istow,' art thou.
>
> 4.[2] 'twinn with,' part with.
>
> 'Istow a maid, or istow a wife?
>
> Wiltow twinn with thy maidenhead, or thy sweet life?'

5.

'O kind sir, if I hae't at my will,

I'll twinn with my life, keep my maidenhead still.'

6.

He's taen out his wee pen-knife,

He's twinned this young lady of her sweet life.

7.

He wiped his knife along the dew;

But the more he wiped, the redder it grew.

8.

The second of them she's to the wood gane,

To seek her old sister, and to bring her hame.

9.

There she met with an outlyer bold,

Lies many long nights in the woods so cold.

10.

'Istow a maid, or istow a wife?

Wiltow twinn with thy maidenhead, or thy sweet life?'

11.

'O kind sir, if I hae't at my will,

I'll twinn with my life, keep my maidenhead still.'

12.

He's taen out his wee pen-knife,

He's twinned this young lady of her sweet life.

13.

He wiped his knife along the dew;

But the more he wiped, the redder it grew.

14.

The youngest o' them she's to the wood gane,

To seek her two sisters, and to bring them hame.

15.

There she met with an outlyer bold,

Lies many long nights in the woods so cold.

16.

'Istow a maid, or istow a wife?

Wiltow twinn with thy maidenhead, or thy sweet life?'

17.

17.² 'speer,' ask.

'If my three brethren they were here,

Such questions as these thou durst nae speer.'

18.

'Pray, what may thy three brethren be,

That I durst na mak' so bold with thee?'

19.

'The eldest o' them is a minister bred,

He teaches the people from evil to good.

20.

'The second o' them is a ploughman good,

He ploughs the land for his livelihood.

21.

'The youngest of them is an outlyer bold,

Lies many a long night in the woods so cold.'

22.

He stuck his knife then into the ground,

He took a long race, let himself fall on.

MARY HAMILTON

THE TEXT given here is from Sharpe's *Ballad Book* (1824). Professor Child collected and printed some twenty-eight variants and fragments, of which none is entirely satisfactory, as regards the telling of the story. The present text will suit our purpose as well as any other, and it ends impressively with the famous pathetic verse of the four Maries.

THE STORY.—Lesley in his *History of Scotland* (1830) says that when Mary Stuart was sent to France in 1548, she had in attendance 'sundry gentlewomen and noblemen's sons and daughters, almost of her own age, of the which there were four in special of whom everyone of them bore the same name of Mary, being of four sundry honourable houses, to wit, Fleming, Livingston, Seton, and Beaton of Creich.' The four Maries were still with the Queen in 1564. Hamilton and Carmichael appear in the ballad in place of Fleming and Livingston.

Scott attributed the origin of the ballad to an incident related by Knox in his *History of the Reformation*: in 1563 or 1564 a Frenchwoman was seduced by the Queen's apothecary, and the babe murdered by consent of father and mother. But the cries of a new-born babe had been heard; search was made, and both parents were 'damned to be hanged upon the public street of Edinburgh.'

In 1824, in his preface to the *Ballad Book*, Charles Kirkpatrick Sharpe produced a similar story from the Russian court. In 1885 this story was retold from authentic sources as follows. After the marriage of one of the ministers of Peter the Great's father with a Hamilton, the Scottish family ranked with the Russian aristocracy. The Czar Peter required that all his Empress Catharine's maids-of-honour should be remarkably handsome; and Mary Hamilton, a niece, it is supposed, of the above minister's wife, was appointed on account of her beauty. This Mary Hamilton had an amour with one Orlof, an aide-de-camp to the Czar; a murdered babe was found, the guilt traced to Mary, and she and Orlof sent to prison in April 1718. Orlof was afterwards released; Mary Hamilton was executed on March 14, 1719.

Professor Child, in printing this ballad in 1889, considered the details of the Russian story2 (most of which I have omitted) to be so closely parallel to the Scottish ballad, that he was convinced that the later story was the origin of the ballad, and that the ballad-maker had located it in Mary Stuart's court on his own responsibility. In September 1895 Mr. Andrew Lang contributed the results of his researches concerning the ballad to *Blackwood's*

Magazine, maintaining that the ballad must have arisen from the 1563 story, as it is too old and too good to have been written since 1718. Balancing this improbability—that the details of a Russian court scandal of 1718 should exactly correspond to a previously extant Scottish ballad—against the improbability of the eighteenth century producing such a ballad, Child afterwards concluded the latter to be the greater. The coincidence is undoubtedly striking; but neither the story nor the name are uncommon.

It is, of course, possible that the story is older than 1563—it should not be difficult to find more than one instance—and that it was first adapted to the 1563 incident and afterwards to the Russian scandal, the two versions being subsequently confused. But there is no evidence for this.

2. See Waliszewski's *Peter the Great* (translated by Lady Mary Loyd), vol. i. p. 251. London, 1897.

MARY HAMILTON

1.

WORD's gane to the kitchen,

And word's gane to the ha',

That Marie Hamilton gangs wi' bairn

To the hichest Stewart of a'.

2.

He's courted her in the kitchen,

He's courted her in the ha',

He's courted her in the laigh cellar,

And that was warst of a'.

3.

She's tyed it in her apron

And she's thrown it in the sea;

Says, 'Sink ye, swim ye, bonny wee babe,

You'll ne'er get mair o' me.'

4.

Down then cam the auld queen,

Goud tassels tying her hair:

'O Marie, where's the bonny wee babe
That I heard greet sae sair?'

5.

'There was never a babe intill my room,
As little designs to be;
It was but a touch o' my sair side,
Come o'er my fair bodie.'

6.

'O Marie, put on your robes o' black,
Or else your robes o' brown,
For ye maun gang wi' me the night,
To see fair Edinbro' town.'

7.

'I winna put on my robes o' black,
Nor yet my robes o' brown;
But I'll put on my robes o' white,
To shine through Edinbro' town.'

8.

When she gaed up the Cannogate,
She laugh'd loud laughters three;
But whan she cam down the Cannogate
The tear blinded her ee.

9.

When she gaed up the Parliament stair,
The heel cam aff her shee;
And lang or she cam down again
She was condemn'd to dee.

10.

When she cam down the Cannogate,

The Cannogate sae free,

Many a ladie look'd o'er her window,

Weeping for this ladie.

11.

'Ye need nae weep for me,' she says,

'Ye need nae weep for me;

For had I not slain mine own sweet babe,

This death I wadna dee.

12.

'Bring me a bottle of wine,' she says,

'The best that e'er ye hae,

That I may drink to my weil-wishers,

And they may drink to me.

13.

'Here's a health to the jolly sailors,

That sail upon the main;

Let them never let on to my father and mother

But what I'm coming hame.

14.

'Here's a health to the jolly sailors,

That sail upon the sea;

Let them never let on to my father and mother

That I cam here to dee.

15.

'Oh little did my mother think,

The day she cradled me,

What lands I was to travel through,

What death I was to dee.

16.

'Oh little did my father think,
The day he held up me,
What lands I was to travel through,
What death I was to dee.

17.

'Last night I wash'd the queen's feet,
And gently laid her down;
And a' the thanks I've gotten the nicht
To be hang'd in Edinbro' town!

18.

'Last nicht there was four Maries,
The nicht there'll be but three;
There was Marie Seton, and Marie Beton,
And Marie Carmichael, and me.'

KINMONT WILLIE

THE TEXT.—There is only one text of this ballad, and that was printed by Scott in the *Minstrelsy* from 'tradition in the West Borders'; he adds that 'some conjectural emendations have been absolutely necessary,' a remark suspicious in itself; and such modernities as the double rhymes in 26.³, 28.³, etc., do not restore confidence.

THE STORY.—The forcible entry into Carlisle Castle and the rescue of William Armstrong, called Will of Kinmouth, took place on April 13, 1596; but Kinmont Willie was notorious as a border thief at least as early as 1584.

The events leading up to the beginning of the ballad were as follow: 'The keen Lord Scroop' was Warden of the West-Marches of England, and 'the bauld Buccleuch' (Sir Walter Scott of Branxholm, or 'Branksome Ha',' 8.²) was the Keeper of Liddesdale. To keep a periodical day of truce, these two sent their respective deputies, the 'fause Sakelde' (or Salkeld) and a certain Robert Scott. In the latter's company was Kinmont Willie. Business being concluded, Kinmont Willie took his leave, and made his way along the Scottish side of the Liddel river, which at that point is the boundary between England and Scotland. The English deputy and his party spied him from their side of the stream; and bearing an ancient grudge against him as a notorious cattle-lifter and thief, they pursued and captured him, and he was placed in the castle of Carlisle.

This brings us to the ballad. 'Hairibee' (1.⁴) is the place of execution at Carlisle. The 'Liddel-rack' in 3.⁴ is a ford over the Liddel river. Branxholm, the Keeper's Hall (8.²) and Stobs (16.⁴) are both within a few miles of Hawick.

The remark in 16.² appears to be untrue: the party that accompanied Buccleuch certainly contained several Armstrongs, including four sons of Kinmont Willie, and 'Dickie of Dryhope' (24.³) was also of that ilk; as well as two Elliots, though not Sir Gilbert, and four Bells. 'Red Rowan' was probably a Forster.

The tune blown on the Warden's trumpets (31.³,⁴) is said to be a favourite song in Liddesdale. See Chambers's *Book of Days*, i. 200.

KINMONT WILLIE

    1.

    O HAVE ye na heard o' the fause Sakelde?

    O have ye na heard o' the keen Lord Scroop?

How they hae taen bauld Kinmont Willie,

On Hairibee to hang him up?

2.

Had Willie had but twenty men,

But twenty men as stout as he,

Fause Sakelde had never the Kinmont taen,

Wi' eight score in his companie.

3.

They band his legs beneath the steed,

They tied his hands behind his back;

They guarded him, fivesome on each side,

And they brought him ower the Liddel-rack.

4.

They led him thro' the Liddel-rack,

And also thro' the Carlisle sands;

They brought him to Carlisle castell,

To be at my Lord Scroop's commands.

5.

'My hands are tied, but my tongue is free,

And whae will dare this deed avow?

Or answer by the Border law?

Or answer to the bauld Buccleuch!'

6.

6.[1] 'haud,' hold: 'reiver,' robber.

'Now haud thy tongue, thou rank reiver!

There's never a Scot shall set ye free;

Before ye cross my castle-yate,

I trow ye shall take farewell o' me.'

7.

7.[4] 'lawing,' reckoning.

'Fear na ye that, my lord,' quo' Willie;

'By the faith o' my body, Lord Scroop,' he said,

'I never yet lodged in a hostelrie,

But I paid my lawing before I gaed.'

8.

Now word is gane to the bauld Keeper,

In Branksome Ha' where that he lay,

That Lord Scroop has taen the Kinmont Willie,

Between the hours of night and day.

9.

He has taen the table wi' his hand,

He garr'd the red wine spring on hie;

'Now Christ's curse on my head,' he said,

'But avenged of Lord Scroop I'll be!

10.

10.[1] 'basnet,' helmet: 'curch,' kerchief.

10.[4] 'lightly,' insult.

'O is my basnet a widow's curch,

Or my lance a wand of the willow-tree,

Or my arm a ladye's lilye hand,

That an English lord should lightly me?

11.

'And have they taen him, Kinmont Willie,

Against the truce of Border tide,

And forgotten that the bauld Buccleuch

Is keeper here on the Scottish side?

12.

'And have they e'en taen him, Kinmont Willie,

Withouten either dread or fear,

And forgotten that the bauld Buccleuch

Can back a steed, or shake a spear?

13.

13.3 'slight,' destroy.

'O were there war between the lands,

As well I wot that there is none,

I would slight Carlisle castell high,

Tho' it were builded of marble stone.

14.

14.1 'low,' fire.

'I would set that castell in a low,

And sloken it with English blood;

There's nevir a man in Cumberland

Should ken where Carlisle castell stood.

15.

'But since nae war's between the lands,

And there is peace, and peace should be,

I'll neither harm English lad or lass,

And yet the Kinmont freed shall be!'

16.

He has call'd him forty marchmen bauld,

I trow they were of his ain name,

Except Sir Gilbert Elliot, call'd

The Laird of Stobs, I mean the same.

17.

17.3 'splent on spauld,' plate-armour on their shoulders.

He has call'd him forty marchmen bauld,

Were kinsmen to the bauld Buccleuch,
With spur on heel, and splent on spauld,
And gleuves of green, and feathers blue.

18.

They were five and five before them a',
Wi' hunting-horns and bugles bright;
And five and five came wi' Buccleuch,
Like Warden's men, arrayed for fight.

19.

19.[3] 'broken men,' outlaws.

And five and five like a mason-gang,
That carried the ladders lang and hie;
And five and five like broken men;
And so they reached the Woodhouselee.

20.

And as we cross'd the Bateable Land,
When to the English side we held,
The first o' men that we met wi',
Whae should it be but fause Sakelde!

21.

'Where be ye gaun, ye hunters keen?'
Quo' fause Sakelde; 'come tell to me!'
'We go to hunt an English stag,
Has trespass'd on the Scots countrie.'

22.

'Where be ye gaun, ye marshal-men?'
Quo' fause Sakelde; 'come tell me true!'
'We go to catch a rank reiver,
Has broken faith wi' the bauld Buccleuch.

- 58 -

23.

'Where are ye gaun, ye mason-lads,
Wi' a' your ladders lang and hie?'
'We gang to herry a corbie's nest,
That wons not far frae Woodhouselee.'

24.

24.⁴ 'lear,' information.

'Where be ye gaun, ye broken men?'
Quo' fause Sakelde; 'come tell to me!'
Now Dickie of Dryhope led that band,
And the nevir a word o' lear had he.

25.

25.² 'Row,' rough.

'Why trespass ye on the English side?
Row-footed outlaws, stand!' quo' he;
The neer a word had Dickie to say,
Sae he thrust the lance thro' his fause bodie.

26.

26.³ 'spait,' flood.

Then on we held for Carlisle toun,
And at Staneshaw-bank the Eden we cross'd;
The water was great, and meikle of spait,
But the nevir a horse nor man we lost.

27.

And when we reach'd the Staneshaw-bank,
The wind was rising loud and hie;
And there the laird garr'd leave our steeds,
For fear that they should stamp and nie.

28.

And when we left the Staneshaw-bank,
The wind began full loud to blaw;
But 'twas wind and weet, and fire and sleet,
When we came beneath the castel-wa'.
29.
We crept on knees, and held our breath,
Till we placed the ladders against the wa';
And sae ready was Buccleuch himsell
To mount the first before us a'.
30.
He has taen the watchman by the throat,
He flung him down upon the lead:
'Had there not been peace between our lands,
Upon the other side thou hadst gaed.
31.
'Now sound out, trumpets!' quo' Buccleuch;
'Let's waken Lord Scroop right merrilie!'
Then loud the Warden's trumpets blew
'Oh whae dare meddle wi' me?'
32.
Then speedilie to wark we gaed,
And raised the slogan ane and a',
And cut a hole thro' a sheet of lead,
And so we wan to the castel-ha'.
33.
33.4 'stear,' stir, disturbance.
They thought King James and a' his men
Had won the house wi' bow and spear;
It was but twenty Scots and ten,

That put a thousand in sic a stear!

34.

34.¹ 'forehammers,' sledge-hammers.

Wi' coulters and wi' forehammers,
We garr'd the bars bang merrilie,
Untill we came to the inner prison,
Where Willie o' Kinmont he did lie.

35.

And when we cam to the lower prison,
Where Willie o' Kinmont he did lie:
'O sleep ye, wake ye, Kinmont Willie,
Upon the morn that thou's to die?'

36.

'O I sleep saft, and I wake aft,
It's lang since sleeping was fleyed frae me;
Gie my service back to my wyfe and bairns,
And a' gude fellows that speer for me.'

37.

Then Red Rowan has hente him up,
The starkest man in Teviotdale:
'Abide, abide now, Red Rowan,
Till of my Lord Scroop I take farewell.

38.

38.³ 'maill,' rent.

'Farewell, farewell, my gude Lord Scroop!
My gude Lord Scroop, farewell!' he cried;
'I'll pay you for my lodging-maill
When first we meet on the border-side.'

39.

Then shoulder high, with shout and cry,
We bore him down the ladder lang;
At every stride Red Rowan made,
I wot the Kinmont's airns play'd clang.

40.

'O mony a time,' quo' Kinmont Willie,
'I have ridden horse baith wild and wood;
But a rougher beast than Red Rowan
I ween my legs have ne'er bestrode.

41.

'And mony a time,' quo' Kinmont Willie,
'I've pricked a horse out oure the furs;
But since the day I backed a steed,
I never wore sic cumbrous spurs.'

42.

We scarce had won the Staneshaw-bank,
When a' the Carlisle bells were rung,
And a thousand men, in horse and foot,
Cam' wi' the keen Lord Scroop along.

43.

Buccleuch has turned to Eden Water,
Even where it flow'd frae bank to brim,
And he has plunged in wi' a' his band,
And safely swam them thro' the stream.

44.

He turned him on the other side,
And at Lord Scroop his glove flung he:
'If ye like na my visit in merry England,
In fair Scotland come visit me!'

45.

45.[3] 'trew,' believe.

All sore astonished stood Lord Scroop,
He stood as still as rock of stane;
He scarcely dared to trew his eyes,
When thro' the water they had gane.
46.
'He is either himsell a devil frae hell,
Or else his mother a witch maun be;
I wad na have ridden that wan water
For a' the gowd in Christentie.'

THE LAIRD O' LOGIE

THE TEXT is that of Scott's *Minstrelsy*, which was repeated in Motherwell's collection, with the insertion of one stanza, obtained from tradition, between Scott's 2 and 3.

THE STORY as told in this variant of the ballad is remarkably true to the historical facts.

The Laird was John Wemyss, younger of Logie, a gentleman-in-waiting to King James VI. of Scotland, and an adherent of the notorious Francis Stuart, Earl of Bothwell. After the failure of the two rash attempts of Bothwell upon the King's person—the former at Holyrood House in 1591 and the second at Falkland in 1592—the Earl persuaded the Laird of Logie and the Laird of Burleigh to join him in a third attempt, which was fixed for the 7th or 9th of August 1592; but the King got wind of the affair, and the two Lairds were seized by the Duke of Lennox and 'committed to ward within Dalkeith.'

The heroine of the ballad was a Danish maid-of-honour to James's Queen; her name is variously recorded as Margaret Vinstar, Weiksterne, Twynstoun, or Twinslace. 'Carmichael' was Sir John Carmichael, appointed captain of the King's guard in 1588.

The ballad stops short at the escape of the lovers by ship. But history relates that the young couple were befriended by the Queen, who refused to comply with the King's demand that May Margaret should be dismissed. Eventually both were received into favour again, though the Laird of Logie was constantly in political trouble. He died in 1599. (See a paper by A. Francis Steuart in *The Scots Magazine* for October 1899, p. 387.)

THE LAIRD O' LOGIE

1.

I WILL sing, if ye will hearken,

If ye will hearken unto me;

The king has ta'en a poor prisoner,

The wanton laird o' young Logie.

2.

Young Logie's laid in Edinburgh chapel,

Carmichael's the keeper o' the key;

And May Margaret's lamenting sair,

A' for the love of Young Logie.

3.

'Lament, lament na, May Margaret,

And of your weeping let me be,

For ye maun to the king himsell,

To seek the life of Young Logie.'

4.

May Margaret has kilted her green cleiding,

And she has curl'd back her yellow hair;

'If I canna get Young Logie's life,

Farewell to Scotland for evermair!'

5.

When she came before the king,

She knelit lowly on her knee;

'O what's the matter, May Margaret?

And what needs a' this courtesie?'

6.

'A boon, a boon, my noble liege,

A boon, a boon, I beg o' thee!

And the first boon that I come to crave,

Is to grant me the life o' Young Logie.'

7.

'O na, O na, May Margaret,

Forsooth, and so it mauna be;

For a' the gowd o' fair Scotland

Shall not save the life o' Young Logie.'

8.

8.[1] 'redding-kaim,' dressing-comb.

But she has stown the king's redding-kaim,
Likewise the queen her wedding knife;
And sent the tokens to Carmichael,
To cause Young Logie get his life.
9.
She sent him a purse o' the red gowd,
Another o' the white monie;
She sent him a pistol for each hand,
And bade him shoot when he gat free.
10.
When he came to the Tolbooth stair,
There he let his volley flee;
It made the king in his chamber start,
E'en in the bed where he might be.
11.
'Gae out, gae out, my merrymen a',
And bid Carmichael come speak to me,
For I'll lay my life the pledge o' that,
That yon's the shot o' Young Logie.'
12.
When Carmichael came before the king,
He fell low down upon his knee;
The very first word that the king spake,
Was 'Where's the laird of Young Logie?'
13.
Carmichael turn'd him round about,
I wat the tear blinded his eye;
'There came a token frae your grace,
Has ta'en away the laird frae me.'

14.
'Hast thou play'd me that, Carmichael?
And hast thou play'd me that?' quoth he;
'The morn the Justice Court's to stand,
And Logie's place ye maun supplie.'
15.
Carmichael's awa to Margaret's bower,
Even as fast as he may dree;
'O if Young Logie be within,
Tell him to come and speak with me.'
16.
May Margaret turn'd her round about,
I wat a loud laugh laughed she;
'The egg is chipp'd, the bird is flown,
Ye'll see nae mair of Young Logie.'
17.
The tane is shipped at the pier of Leith,
The tother at the Queen's Ferrie;
And she's gotten a father to her bairn,
The wanton laird of Young Logie.

CAPTAIN CAR

THE TEXT is from a Cottonian MS. of the sixteenth century in the British Museum (Vesp. A. xxv. fol. 178). It is carelessly written, and words are here and there deleted and altered. I have allowed myself the liberty of choosing readings from several alternatives or possibilities.

THE STORY.—There seems to be no doubt that this ballad is founded upon an historical incident of 1571. The Scottish variants are mostly called *Edom o' Gordon*, *i.e.* Adam Gordon, who was brother to George Gordon, Earl of Huntly. Adam was a bold soldier; and, his clan being at variance with the Forbeses—on religious grounds,—he encountered them twice in the autumn of 1571, and inflicted severe defeat on them at the battles of Tuiliangus and Crabstane. In November he approached the castle of Towie, a stronghold of the Forbes clan; but the lady occupying it obstinately refused to yield it up, and it was burnt to the ground.

It is not clear whether the responsibility of giving the order to fire the castle attaches to Adam Gordon or to Captain Car or Ker, who was Adam's right-hand man. But when all is said on either side, it is irrational, as Child points out, to apply modern standards of morality or expediency to sixteenth-century warfare. It is curious that this text, almost contemporary with the occurrence which gave rise to the ballad, should be wholly concerned with Captain Car and make no mention of Adam Gordon.

For the burden, see Chappell *Popular Music of the Olden Time*, i. 226.

CAPTAIN CAR

    1.

    IT befell at Martynmas,

    When wether waxed colde,

    Captaine Care said to his men,

    'We must go take a holde.'

    Burden.[1] 'to-towe' = too-too.

    Syck, sicke, and to-towe sike,

    And sicke and like to die;

    The sikest nighte that ever I abode,

    God lord have mercy on me!

2.
'Haille, master, and wether you will,
And wether ye like it best;'
'To the castle of Crecrynbroghe,
And there we will take our reste.'

3.
'I knowe wher is a gay castle,
Is builded of lyme and stone;
Within their is a gay ladie,
Her lord is riden and gone.'

4.
The ladie she lend on her castle-walle,
She loked upp and downe;
There was she ware of an host of men,
Come riding to the towne.

5.
'Se yow, my meri men all,
And se yow what I see?
Yonder I see an host of men,
I muse who they bee.'

6.
She thought he had ben her wed lord,
As he com'd riding home;
Then was it traitur Captaine Care
The lord of Ester-towne.

7.
They wer no soner at supper sett,
Then after said the grace,
Or Captaine Care and all his men

Wer lighte aboute the place.

8.

8.² 'bande,' bond, compact.

8.⁴ 'ere,' plough.

'Gyve over thi howsse, thou lady gay,

And I will make the a bande;

To-nighte thou shall ly within my armes,

To-morrowe thou shall ere my lande.'

9.

Then bespacke the eldest sonne,

That was both whitt and redde:

'O mother dere, geve over your howsse,

Or elles we shalbe deade.'

10.

'I will not geve over my hous,' she saithe,

'Not for feare of my lyffe;

It shalbe talked throughout the land,

The slaughter of a wyffe.'

11.

11.¹ 'pestilett,' pistolet.

'Fetch me my pestilett,

And charge me my gonne,

That I may shott at yonder bloddy butcher,

The lord of Easter-towne.'

12.

Styfly upon her wall she stode,

And lett the pellettes flee;

But then she myst the blody bucher,

And she slew other three.

13.

['I will] not geve over my hous,' she saithe,

'Netheir for lord nor lowne;

Nor yet for traitour Captain Care,

The lord of Easter-towne.

14.

14.⁴ 'eare,' and 18.⁴ 'ayre,' both = heir.

'I desire of Captine Care

And all his bloddye band,

That he would save my eldest sonne,

The eare of all my lande.'

15.

'Lap him in a shete,' he sayth,

'And let him downe to me,

And I shall take him in my armes,

His waran shall I be.'

16.

The captayne sayd unto him selfe:

Wyth sped, before the rest,

He cut his tonge out of his head,

His hart out of his breast.

17.

He lapt them in a handkerchef,

And knet it of knotes three,

And cast them over the castell-wall,

At that gay ladye.

18.

'Fye upon the, Captayne Care,

And all thy bloddy band!

For thou hast slayne my eldest sonne,

The ayre of all my land.'

19.

Then bespake the yongest sonne,

That sat on the nurse's knee,

Sayth, 'Mother gay, geve over your house;

It smoldereth me.'

20.

'I wold geve my gold,' she saith,

'And so I wolde my ffee,

For a blaste of the westryn wind,

To dryve the smoke from thee.

21.

'Fy upon the, John Hamleton,

That ever I paid the hyre!

For thou hast broken my castle-wall,

And kyndled in the ffyre.'

22.

The lady gate to her close parler,

The fire fell aboute her head;

She toke up her children thre,

Seth, 'Babes, we are all dead.'

23.

Then bespake the hye steward,

That is of hye degree;

Saith, 'Ladie gay, you are in close,

Wether ye fighte or flee.'

24.

Lord Hamleton drem'd in his dream,

In Carvall where he laye,

His halle were all of fyre,

His ladie slayne or daye.

25.

25.¹ 'Busk and bowne,' make ready.

'Busk and bowne, my mery men all,

Even and go ye with me;

For I drem'd that my hall was on fyre,

My lady slayne or day.'

26.

26.⁴ 'no dele,' in no way. Cf. *somedele*, etc.

He buskt him and bown'd hym,

And like a worthi knighte;

And when he saw his hall burning,

His harte was no dele lighte.

27.

He sett a trumpett till his mouth,

He blew as it ples'd his grace;

Twenty score of Hamlentons

Was light aboute the place.

28.

28.⁴ 'quite,' acquitted, unpunished.

'Had I knowne as much yesternighte

As I do to-daye,

Captaine Care and all his men

Should not have gone so quite.

29.

'Fye upon the, Captaine Care,

And all thy blody bande!

Thou haste slayne my lady gay,

More wurth then all thy lande.

30.

30.[1] 'ought,' owed.

'If thou had ought eny ill will,' he saith,

'Thou shoulde have taken my lyffe,

And have saved my children thre,

All and my lovesome wyffe.'

SIR PATRICK SPENCE

THE TEXT is taken from Percy's *Reliques* (1765), vol. i. p. 71, 'given from two MS. copies, transmitted from Scotland.' Herd had a very similar ballad, which substitutes a Sir Andrew Wood for the hero. The version of this ballad printed in most collections is that of Scott's *Minstrelsy*, Sir Patrick Spens being the spelling adopted.3 Scott compounded his ballad of two manuscript copies and a few verses from recitation, but the result is of unnecessary length.

THE STORY.—Much labour has been expended upon the question whether this ballad has an historical basis or not. From Percy's ballad—the present text—we can gather that Sir Patrick Spence was chosen by the king to convey something of value to a certain destination; and later versions tell us that the ship is bound for Norway, the object of the voyage being either to bring home the king of Norway's daughter, or the Scottish king's daughter, or to take out the Scottish king's daughter to be queen in Norway. The last variation can be supported by history, Margaret, daughter of Alexander III. of Scotland, being married in 1281 to Erik, king of Norway. Many of the knights and nobles who accompanied her to Norway were drowned on the voyage home.

However, we need not elaborate our researches in the attempt to prove that the ballad is historical. It is certainly of English and Scottish origin, and has no parallels in the ballads of other lands. 'Haf owre to Aberdour,' *i.e.* halfway between Aberdour in Buchan and the coast of Norway, lies the island of Papa Stronsay, on which there is a tumulus called 'the Earl's Knowe' (knoll); but the tradition, that this marks the grave of Sir Patrick Spence, is in all probability a modern invention.

3. Coleridge, however, wrote of the 'grand old ballad of Sir Patrick Spence.'

SIR PATRICK SPENCE

    1.

    1.[1] 'Dumferling,' *i.e.* Dunfermline, on the north side of the Firth of Forth.

    THE king sits in Dumferling toune,

    Drinking the blude-reid wine:

    'O whar will I get [a] guid sailor,

To sail this schip of mine?'

2.

Up and spak an eldern knicht,

Sat at the king's richt kne:

'Sir Patrick Spence is the best sailor

That sails upon the se.'

3.

The king has written a braid letter,

And sign'd it wi' his hand,

And sent it to Sir Patrick Spence,

Was walking on the sand.

4.

The first line that Sir Patrick red,

A loud lauch lauched he;

The next line that Sir Patrick red,

The teir blinded his ee.

5.

'O wha is this has done this deid,

This ill deid don to me,

To send me out this time o' the yeir,

To sail upon the se!

6.

'Mak haste, mak haste, my mirry men all,

Our guid schip sails the morne:'

'O say na sae, my master deir,

Fir I feir a deadlie storme.

7.

'Late, late yestreen I saw the new moone

Wi' the auld moone in hir arme,

And I feir, I feir, my deir master,
That we will cum to harme.'

8.

O our Scots nobles wer richt laith
To weet their cork-heil'd schoone;
Bot lang owre a' the play wer play'd,
Thair hats they swam aboone.

9.

O lang, lang may their ladies sit
Wi' thair fans into their hand
Or eir they se Sir Patrick Spence
Cum sailing to the land.

10.

O lang, lang may the ladies stand,
Wi' thair gold kerns in their hair,
Waiting for thair ain deir lords,
For they'll se thame na mair.

11.

Haf owre, haf owre to Aberdour,
It's fiftie fadom deip,
And thair lies guid Sir Patrick Spence,
Wi' the Scots lords at his feit.

FLODDEN FIELD

THE TEXT is from Thomas Deloney's *Pleasant History of John Winchcomb*,4 the eighth edition of which, in 1619, is the earliest known. 'In disgrace of the Soots,' says Deloney, 'and in remembrance of the famous atchieved historie, the commons of England made this song, which to this day is not forgotten of many.' I suspect it was Deloney himself rather than the commons of England who made this song. A variant is found in Additional MS. 32,380 in the British Museum—a statement which might be of interest if it were not qualified by the addition 'formerly in the possession of J. Payne Collier.' That egregious antiquary took the pains to fill the blank leaves of a sixteenth-century manuscript with ballads either copied from their original sources, as this from Deloney, or forged by Collier himself; he then made a transcript in his own handwriting (Add. MS. 32,381), and finally printed selections. In the present ballad he has inserted two or three verses of his own; otherwise the changes from Deloney's ballad are slight.

A very long ballad on the same subject is in the Percy Folio, and similar copies in Harleian MSS. 293 and 367. Another is 'Scotish Field,' also in the Percy Folio.

THE STORY.—Lesley says in his History, 'This battle was called the Field of Flodden by the Scotsmen and Brankston [Bramstone, 8.3] by the Englishmen, because it was stricken on the hills of Flodden beside a town called Brankston; and was stricken the ninth day of September, 1513.'

The ballad follows history closely. 'Lord Thomas Howard' (6.1), uncle to the queen, escorted her to Scotland in 1503: 'This is ground enough,' says Child, 'for the ballad's making him her chamberlain ten years later.'

'Jack with a feather' (12.1) is a contemptuous phrase directed at King James's rashness.

4. Reprinted from the ninth edition of 1633 by J. O. Halliwell [-Phillipps], 1859, where the ballad appears on pp. 48-9. Deloney's book was licensed in 1597.

FLODDEN FIELD

1.

KING Jamie hath made a vow,

Keep it well if he may!

That he will be at lovely London

Upon Saint James his day.

2.

'Upon Saint James his day at noon,
At fair London will I be,
And all the lords in merry Scotland,
They shall dine there with me.'

3.

Then bespake good Queen Margaret,
The tears fell from her eye:
'Leave off these wars, most noble king,
Keep your fidelity.

4.

'The water runs swift and wondrous deep,
From bottom unto the brim;
My brother Henry hath men good enough;
England is hard to win.'

5.

'Away,' quoth he, 'with this silly fool!
In prison fast let her lie:
For she is come of the English blood,
And for those words she shall die.'

6.

With that bespake Lord Thomas Howard,
The queen's chamberlain that day:
'If that you put Queen Margaret to death,
Scotland shall rue it alway.'

7.

7.[2] 'Mome,' dolt.
Then in a rage King James did say,

'Away with this foolish mome!

He shall be hanged, and the other be burned,

So soon as I come home.'

8.

At Flodden Field the Scots came in,

Which made our English men fain;

At Bramstone Green this battle was seen,

There was King Jamie slain.

9.

Then presently the Scots did fly,

Their cannons they left behind;

Their ensigns gay were won all away,

Our soldiers did beat them blind.

10.

To tell you plain, twelve thousand were slain

That to the fight did stand,

And many prisoners took that day,

The best in all Scotland.

11.

That day made many [a] fatherless child,

And many a widow poor,

And many a Scottish gay lady

Sat weeping in her bower.

12.

Jack with a feather was lapt all in leather,

His boastings were all in vain;

He had such a chance, with a new morrice dance,

He never went home again.

DICK O' THE COW

THE TEXT is a combination of three, but mainly from a text which seems to have been sent to Percy in 1775. The other two are from Scottish tradition of the late eighteenth and early nineteenth centuries. I have made a few changes in spelling only. The ballad was certainly known before the end of the sixteenth century, as Thomas Nashe refers to it in 1596:—'*Dick of the Cow*, that mad Demilance Northren Borderer, who plaid his prizes with the Lord *Iockey* so brauely' (Nashe's *Works*, ed. R. B. McKerrow, iii. p. 5). *Dick at the Caw* occurs in a list of 'penny merriments' printed for, and sold by, Philip Brooksby, about 1685.

THE STORY is yet another of the Border ballads of the Armstrongs and Liddesdale, and tells itself in an admirable way.

The 'Cow,' of course, cannot refer to cattle, as the word would be 'Kye': possibly it means 'broom,' or the hut in which he lived. See Murray's *Dictionary*, and cp. 9.[3]

'Billie' means 'brother'; hence the quaint 'billie Willie.' It is the same word as 'bully,' used of Bottom the Weaver, which also occurs in the ballad of *Bewick and Grahame*, 5.[2] (see p. 102 of this volume).

DICK O' THE COW

    1.

    1.[3] 'lidder,' lazy.

    NOW Liddisdale has long lain in,

    Fa la

    There is no rideing there at a';

    Fa la

    Their horse is growing so lidder and fatt

    That are lazie in the sta'.

    Fa la la didle

    2.

    2.[2] 'billie,' brother.

    2.[3] 'feed,' feud.

    Then Johnë Armstrang to Willie can say,

'Billie, a rideing then will we;

England and us has been long at a feed;

Perhaps we may hitt of some bootie.'

3.

Then they're com'd on to Hutton Hall,

They rade that proper place about;

But the laird he was the wiser man,

For he had left nae gear without.

4.

Then he had left nae gear to steal,

Except six sheep upon a lee;

Says Johnie, 'I'de rather in England die,

Before their six sheep goed to Liddisdale with me.

5.

5.² 'know,' hillock.

'But how cal'd they the man we last with mett,

Billie, as we came over the know?'

'That same he is an innocent fool,

And some men calls him Dick o' the Cow.'

6.

'That fool has three as good kyne of his own

As is in a' Cumberland, billie,' quoth he;

'Betide my life, betide my death,

These three kyne shal go to Liddisdaile with me.'

7.

Then they're com'd on to the poor fool's house,

And they have broken his wals so wide;

They have loos'd out Dick o' the Cow's kyne three,

And tane three co'erlets off his wife's bed.

8.

Then on the morn, when the day grew light,

The shouts and crys rose loud and high;

'Hold thy tongue, my wife,' he says,

'And of thy crying let me bee.

9.

'Hald thy tongue, my wife,' he says,

'And of thy crying let me bee,

And ay that where thou wants a kow,

Good sooth that I shal bring thee three.'

10.

Then Dick's com'd on to lord and master,

And I wat a drerie fool was he;

'Hald thy tongue, my fool,' he says,

'For I may not stand to jest with thee.'

11.

'Shame speed a' your jesting, my lord,' quo' Dickie,

'For nae such jesting 'grees with me;

Liddesdaile has been in my house this last night,

And they have tane my three kyne from me.'

12.

'But I may nae langer in Cumberland dwel,

To be your poor fool and your leel,

Unless ye give me leave, my lord,

To go to Liddisdale and steal.'

13.

'To give thee leave, my fool,' he says,

'Thou speaks against mine honour and me;

Unless thou give me thy troth and thy right hand,

Thou'l steal frae nane but them that sta' from thee.'

14.

'There is my trouth and my right hand;

My head shal hing on Hairibie,

I'le never crose Carlele sands again,

If I steal frae a man but them that sta' frae me.'

15.

Dickie has tane leave at lord and master,

And I wat a merrie fool was he;

He has bought a bridle and a pair of new spurs,

And has packed them up in his breek-thigh.

6.

Then Dickie's come on for Puddinburn,

Even as fast as he may drie;

Dickie's come on for Puddinburn,

Where there was thirty Armstrongs and three.

17.

'What's this com'd on me!' quo' Dickë,

'What meakle wae's this happen'd on me,' quo' he,

'Where here is but an innocent fool,

And there is thirty Armstrongs and three!'

18.

Yet he's com'd up to the hall among them all;

So wel he became his courtisie;

'Well may ye be, my good Laird's Jock,

But the deil bless all your companie!

19.

'I'm come to plain of your man Fair Johnie Armstrong,

And syne his billie Willie,' quo' he;

'How they have been in my house this last night,

And they have tane my three ky frae me.'

20.

20.⁵ 'burden of batts,' all the blows he can bear.

Quo' Johnie Armstrong, 'We'll him hang;'

'Nay,' then quo' Willie, 'we'll him slae;'

But up bespake another young man,

'We'le nit him in a four-nooked sheet,

Give him his burden of batts, and lett him gae.'

21.

Then up bespake the good Laird's Jock,

The best falla in the companie;

'Sitt thy way down a little while, Dickë,

And a peice of thine own cow's hough I'l give to thee.'

22.

22.² 'dought,' was able.

But Dickie's heart it grew so great

That never a bitt of it he dought to eat;

But Dickie was warr of ane auld peat-house,

Where there al the night he thought for to sleep.

23.

Then Dickie was warr of that auld peat-house,

Where there al the night he thought for to ly;

And a' the prayers the poor fool pray'd was,

'I wish I had a mense for my own three kye!'

24.

Then it was the use of Puddinburn,

And the house of Mangertoun, all haile!

These that came not at the first call

They gott no more meat till the next meall.

25.

25.¹ 'aevery,' ravenous.

The lads, that hungry and aevery was,
Above the door-head they flang the key.
Dickie took good notice to that;
Says, 'There's a bootie younder for me.'

26.

26.³ 'St. Mary knot,' a triple knot.

Then Dickie's gane into the stable,
Where there stood thirty horse and three;
He has ty'd them a' with St. Mary knot,
All these horse but barely three.

27.

He has ty'd them a' with St. Mary knot,
All these horse but barely three;
He has loupen on one, taken another in his hand,
And out at the door and gane is Dickie.

28.

Then on the morn, when the day grew light,
The shouts and cryes rose loud and high;
'What's that theife?' quo' the good Laird's Jock,
'Tel me the truth and the verity.

29.

'What's that theife?' quo' the good Laird's Jock,
'See unto me ye do not lie.
Dick o' the Cow has been in the stable this last nicht,
And has my brother's horse and mine frae me.'

30.

'Ye wad never be tel'd it,' quo' the Laird's Jock,

'Have ye not found my tales fu' leel?

Ye wad never out of England bide,

Till crooked and blind and a' wad steal.'

31.

'But will thou lend me thy bay?' Fair Johnë Armstrong can say,

'There's nae mae horse loose in the stable but he;

And I'le either bring ye Dick o' the Kow again.

Or the day is come that he must die.'

32.

32.⁴ The copy reads 'should no make.'

'To lend thee my bay,' the Laird's Jock can say,

'He's both worth gold and good monie;

Dick o' the Kow has away twa horse,

I wish no thou should make him three.'

33.

33.¹ 'jack,' jerkin.

He has tane the Laird's jack on his back,

The twa-handed sword that hang leugh by his thigh;

He has tane the steel cap on his head,

And on is he to follow Dickie.

34.

Then Dickie was not a mile off the town,

I wat a mile but barely three,

Till John Armstrong has o'ertane Dick o' the Kow,

Hand for hand on Cannobie lee.

35.

'Abide thee, bide now, Dickie than,

The day is come that thou must die.'

Dickie looked o'er his left shoulder,

'Johnie, has thou any mo in thy company?

36.

'There is a preacher in our chapell,

And a' the lee-lang day teaches he;

When day is gane, and night is come,

There's never a word I mark but three.

37.

'The first and second's Faith and Conscience,

The third is, Johnie, Take head of thee!

But what faith and conscience had thou, traitor,

When thou took my three kye frae me?

38.

'And when thou had tane my three kye,

Thou thought in thy heart thou was no wel sped;

But thou sent thy billie Willie o'er the know,

And he took three co'erlets off my wife's bed.'

39.

Then Johnë lett a spear fa' leugh by his thigh,

Thought well to run the innocent through,

But the powers above was more than his,

He ran but the poor fool's jerkin through.

40.

40.[1] 'blan,' stopped.

Together they ran or ever they blan;

This was Dickie the fool, and hee;

Dickie could not win to him with the blade of the sword,

But he fel'd him with the plummet under the eye.

41.

Now Dickie has fel'd Fair Johnë Armstrong,

The prettiest man in the south countrey;

'Gramercie,' then can Dickie say,

'I had twa horse, thou has made me three.'

42.

He has tane the laird's jack of his back,

The twa-handed sword that hang leugh by his thigh;

He has tane the steel cap off his head;

'Johnie, I'le tel my master I met with thee.'

43.

When Johnë waken'd out of his dream,

I wat a drery man was he;

'Is thou gane now, Dickie, than?

The shame gae in thy company!

44.

'Is thou gane now, Dickie, than?

The shame go in thy companie!

For if I should live this hundred year,

I shal never fight with a fool after thee.'

45.

Then Dickie comed home to lord and master,

Even as fast as he may drie.

'Now, Dickie, I shal neither eat meat nor drink

Till high hanged that thou shall be!'

46.

'The shame speed the liars, my lord!' quo' Dickie,

'That was no the promise ye made to me;

For I'd never gane to Liddesdale to steal

Till that I sought my leave at thee.'

47.

47.² 'limmer,' rascal.

'But what gart thou steal the Laird's Jock's horse?
And, limmer, what gart thou steal him?' quo' he;
'For lang might thou in Cumberland dwelt
Or the Laird's Jock had stoln ought frae thee.'

48.

'Indeed I wat ye lee'd, my lord,
And even so loud as I hear ye lie;
I wan him frae his man, Fair Johnë Armstrong,
Hand for hand on Cannobie lee.

49.

'There's the jack was on his back,
The twa-handed sword that hung leugh by his thigh;
There's the steel cap was on his head;
I have a' these takens to lett you see.'

50.

'If that be true thou to me tels
(I trow thou dare not tel a lie),
I'le give thee twenty pound for the good horse,
Wel tel'd in thy cloke-lap shall be.

51.

'And I'le give thee one of my best milk-kye
To maintain thy wife and children three;
And that may be as good, I think,
As ony twa o' thine might be.'

52.

'The shame speed the liars, my lord!' quo' Dickie;
'Trow ye ay to make a fool of me?

I'le either have thirty pound for the good horse,

Or else he's gae to Mattan fair wi' me.'

53.

Then he has given him thirty pound for the good horse,

All in gold and good monie:

He has given him one of his best milk-kye

To maintain his wife and children three.

54.

Then Dickie's come down through Carlile town,

Even as fast as he may drie.

The first of men that he with mett

Was my lord's brother, Bailife Glazenberrie.

55.

'Well may ye be, my good Ralph Scrupe!'

'Welcome, my brother's fool!' quo' he;

'Where did thou gett Fair Johnie Armstrong's horse?'

'Where did I get him but steal him,' quo' he.

56.

56.³ I have inserted 'thou' to complete the sense; 'and,' here and below, 60.⁴, meaning 'if.'

'But will thou sell me Fair Johnie Armstrong's horse?

And, billie, will thou sell him to me?' quo' he;

'Ay, and [thou] tel me the monie on my cloke-lap,

For there's not one farthing I'le trust thee.'

57.

'I'le give thee fifteen pound for the good horse,

Wel told on thy cloke-lap shal be;

And I'le give thee one of my best milk-kye

To maintain thy wife and thy children three.'

58.

'The shame speed the liars, my lord!' quo' Dickë,

'Trow ye ay to make a fool of me?' quo' he;

'I'le either have thirty pound for the good horse,

Or else he's to Mattan Fair with me.'

59.

He has given him thirty pound for the good horse,

All in gold and good monie;

He has given him one of his best milk-kye

To maintain his wife and children three.

60.

Then Dickie lap a loup on high,

And I wat a loud laughter leugh he;

'I wish the neck of the third horse were browken,

For I have a better of my own, and onie better can be.'

61.

Then Dickie com'd hame to his wife again.

Judge ye how the poor fool he sped!

He has given her three score of English pounds

For the three auld co'erlets was tane off her bed.

62.

'Hae, take thee there twa as good kye,

I trow, as all thy three might be;

And yet here is a white-footed naigg,

I think he'le carry both thee and me.

63.

'But I may no langer in Cumberland dwell;

The Armstrongs they'le hang me high.'

But Dickie has tane leave at lord and master,

And Burgh under Stanemuir there dwels Dickie.

SIR HUGH IN THE GRIME'S DOWNFALL

THE TEXT given here is comparatively a late one, from the Roxburghe collection (iii. 456). An earlier broadside, in the same and other collections, gives a longer but curiously corrupted version, exhibiting such perversions as 'Screw' for 'Scroop,' and 'Garlard' for 'Carlisle.'

THE STORY in its full form relates that Sir Hugh in the Grime (Hughie Graeme or Graham) stole a mare from the Bishop of Carlisle, by way of retaliation for the Bishop's seduction of his wife. He was pursued by Lord Scroop, taken, and conveyed to Carlisle and hanged.

Scott suggested that Hugh Graham may have been one of four hundred Borderers accused to the Bishop of Carlisle of various murders and thefts about 1548.

SIR HUGH IN THE GRIME'S DOWNFALL

1.

GOOD Lord John is a hunting gone,

Over the hills and dales so far,

For to take Sir Hugh in the Grime,

For stealing of the bishop's mare.

He derry derry down

2.

Hugh in the Grime was taken then

And carried to Carlisle town;

The merry women came out amain,

Saying, 'The name of Grime shall never go down.'

3.

O then a jury of women was brought,

Of the best that could be found;

Eleven of them spoke all at once,

Saying 'The name of Grime shall never go down.'

4.
And then a jury of men was brought,
More the pity for to be!
Eleven of them spoke all at once,
Saying 'Hugh in the Grime, you are guilty.'

5.
Hugh in the Grime was cast to be hang'd,
Many of his friends did for him lack;
For fifteen foot in the prisin he did jump,
With his hands tyed fast behind his back.

6.
Then bespoke our good Lady Ward,
As she set on the bench so high;
'A peck of white pennys I'll give to my lord,
If he'll grant Hugh Grime to me.

7.
'And if it be not full enough,
I'll stroke it up with my silver fan;
And if it be not full enough,
I'll heap it up with my own hand.'

8.
'Hold your tongue now, Lady Ward,
And of your talkitive let it be!
There is never a Grime came in this court
That at thy bidding shall saved be.'

9.
Then bespoke our good Lady Moor,
As she sat on the bench so high;
'A yoke of fat oxen I'll give to my lord,

If he'll grant Hugh Grime to me.'

10.

'Hold your tongue now, good Lady Moor,

And of your talkitive let it be!

There is never a Grime came to this court

That at thy bidding saved shall be.'

11.

Sir Hugh in the Grime look'd out of the door,

With his hand out of the bar;

There he spy'd his father dear,

Tearing of his golden hair.

12.

'Hold your tongue, good father dear,

And of your weeping let it be!

For if they bereave me of my life,

They cannot bereave me of the heavens so high.'

13.

Sir Hugh in the Grime look'd out at the door;

Oh, what a sorry heart had he!

There he spy'd his mother dear,

Weeping and wailing 'Oh, woe is me!'

14.

'Hold your tongue now, mother dear,

And of your weeping let it be!

For if they bereave me of my life,

They cannot bereave me of heaven's fee.

15.
'I'll leave my sword to Johnny Armstrong,
That is made of mettal so fine,
That when he comes to the border-side
He may think of Hugh in the Grime.'

THE DEATH OF PARCY REED

THE TEXT.—There are two texts available for this ballad, of which the second one, here given, was said to have been taken down from the singing of an old woman by James Telfer of Liddesdale, and was so printed in Richardson's *Borderers' Table Book* (1846). It preserves almost the whole of the other version, taken from Robert White's papers, who recorded it in 1829; but it obviously bears marks of having been tampered with by Telfer. However, it contains certain stanzas which Child says may be regarded as traditional, and it is therefore preferred here.

THE STORY.—Percival or Parcy Reed was warden of the district round Troughend, a high tract of land in Redesdale. In the discharge of his duties he incurred the enmity of the family of Hall of Girsonsfield (two miles east of Troughend) and of some moss-troopers named Crosier. As the ballad shows, the treachery of the Halls delivered Parcy Reed into the Crosiers' hands at a hut in Batinghope, a glen westward of the Whitelee stream. Local tradition adds to the details narrated in the ballad that Parcy's wife had been warned by a dream of her husband's danger, and that on the following morning his loaf of bread happened to be turned upside down—a very bad omen.

Further, we learn from the same source, the Crosiers' barbarous treatment of Parcy's corpse aroused the indignation of the neighbourhood, and they and the treacherous Halls were driven away.

Girsonsfield has belonged to no one of the name of Hall as far back as Elizabeth, whence it is argued that the ballad is not later than the sixteenth century.

THE DEATH OF PARCY REED

    1.

    1.[2] 'reaving,' robbing.

    1.[4] 'staig,' horse; 'stot,' ox.

    GOD send the land deliverance

    Frae every reaving, riding Scot!

    We'll sune hae neither cow nor ewe,

    We'll sune hae neither staig nor stot.

    2.

The outlaws come frae Liddesdale,
They herry Redesdale far and near;
The rich man's gelding it maun gang,
They canna pass the puir man's mear.

3.

Sure it were weel, had ilka thief
Around his neck a halter strang;
And curses heavy may they light
On traitors vile oursels amang.

4.

Now Parcy Reed has Crosier taen,
He has delivered him to the law;
But Crosier says he'll do waur than that,
He'll make the tower o' Troughend fa'.

5.

And Crosier says he will do waur,
He will do waur if waur can be;
He'll make the bairns a' fatherless;
And then the land it may lie lee.

6.

'To the hunting, ho!' cried Parcy Reed,
'The morning sun is on the dew;
The cauler breeze frae off the fells
Will lead the dogs to the quarry true.

7.

'To the hunting, ho!' cried Parcy Reed,
And to the hunting he has gane;
And the three fause Ha's o' Girsonsfield
Alang wi' him he has them ta'en.

8.

They hunted high, they hunted low,

By heathery hill and birken shaw;

They raised a buck on Rooken Edge,

And blew the mort at fair Ealylawe.

9.

They hunted high, they hunted low,

They made the echoes ring amain;

With music sweet o' horn and hound,

They merry made fair Redesdale glen.

10.

They hunted high, they hunted low,

They hunted up, they hunted down,

Until the day was past the prime,

And it grew late in the afternoon.

11.

They hunted high in Batinghope,

When as the sun was sinking low.

Says Parcy then, 'Ca' off the dogs,

We'll bait our steeds and homeward go.'

12.

They lighted high in Batinghope,

Atween the brown and benty ground;

They had but rested a little while,

Till Parcy Reed was sleeping sound.

13.

There's nane may lean on a rotten staff,

But him that risks to get a fa';

There's nane may in a traitor trust,

And traitors black were every Ha'.

14.

They've stown the bridle off his steed,

And they've put water in his lang gun;

They've fixed his sword within the sheath,

That out again it winna come.

15.

'Awaken ye, waken ye, Parcy Reed,

Or by your enemies be taen;

For yonder are the five Crosiers

A-coming owre the Hingin-stane.'

16.

'If they be five, and we be four,

Sae that ye stand alang wi' me,

Then every man ye will take one,

And only leave but two to me.

We will them meet as brave men ought,

And make them either fight or flee.'

17.

'We mayna stand, we canna stand,

We daurna stand alang wi' thee;

The Crosiers haud thee at a feud,

And they wad kill baith thee and we.'

18.

'O, turn thee, turn thee, Johnnie Ha',

O, turn thee, man, and fight wi' me;

When ye come to Troughend again,

My gude black naig I will gie thee;

He cost full twenty pound o' gowd,

Atween my brother John and me.'

19.

'I mayna turn, I canna turn,
I daurna turn and fight wi' thee;
The Crosiers haud thee at a feud,
And they wad kill baith thee and me.'

20.

'O, turn thee, turn thee, Willie Ha',
O, turn thee, man, and fight wi' me;
When ye come to Troughend again,
A yoke o' owsen I'll gie thee.'

21.

'I mayna turn, I canna turn,
I daurna turn and fight wi' thee;
The Crosiers haud thee at a feud,
And they wad kill baith thee and me.'

22.

'O, turn thee, turn thee, Tommy Ha',
O, turn now, man, and fight wi' me;
If ever we come to Troughend again,
My daughter Jean I'll gie to thee.'

23.

'I mayna turn, I canna turn,
I daurna turn, and fight wi' thee;
The Crosiers haud thee at a feud,
And they wad kill baith thee and me.'

24.

'O, shame upon ye, traitors a'!
I wish your hames ye may never see;

Ye've stown the bridle off my naig,
And I can neither fight nor flee.

25.

'Ye've stown the bridle off my naig,
And ye've put water i' my lang gun;
Ye've fixed my sword within the sheath,
That out again it winna come.'

26.

26.⁴ 'graithed,' accoutred.

He had but time to cross himsel',
A prayer he hadna time to say,
Till round him came the Crosiers keen,
All riding graithed, and in array.

27.

'Weel met, weel met, now, Parcy Reed,
Thou art the very man we sought;
Owre lang hae we been in your debt,
Now will we pay you as we ought.

28.

28.³ 'fankit,' entangled.

'We'll pay thee at the nearest tree,
Where we shall hang thee like a hound;'
Brave Parcy rais'd his fankit sword,
And fell'd the foremost to the ground.

29.

Alake, and wae for Parcy Reed,
Alake, he was an unarmed man;
Four weapons pierced him all at once,
As they assailed him there and than.

30.

They fell upon him all at once,

They mangled him most cruellie;

The slightest wound might caused his deid,

And they hae gi'en him thirty-three:

They hacket off his hands and feet,

And left him lying on the lee.

31.

31.[4] 'the airt o',' *i.e.* in the direction of.

'Now, Parcy Reed, we've paid our debt,

Ye canna weel dispute the tale,'

The Crosiers said, and off they rade;

They rade the airt o' Liddesdale.

32.

It was the hour o' gloaming gray,

When herds come in frae fauld and pen;

A herd he saw a huntsman lie,

Says he, 'Can this be Laird Troughen'?'

33.

'There's some will ca' me Parcy Reed,

And some will ca' me Laird Troughen';

It's little matter what they ca' me,

My faes hae made me ill to ken.

34.

'There's some will ca' me Parcy Reed,

And speak my praise in tower and town

It's little matter what they do now,

My life-blood rudds the heather brown.

35.

'There's some will ca' me Parcy Reed,
And a' my virtues say and sing;
I would much rather have just now
A draught o' water frae the spring.'
36.
The herd flung aff his clouted shoon,
And to the nearest fountain ran;
He made his bonnet serve a cup,
And wan the blessing o' the dying man.
37.
'Now, honest herd, you maun do mair,—
Ye maun do mair as I you tell;
You maun bear tidings to Troughend,
And bear likewise my last farewell.
38.
'A farewell to my wedded wife,
A farewell to my brother John,
Wha sits into the Troughend tower,
Wi' heart as black as any stone.

39.
'A farewell to my daughter Jean,
A farewell to my young sons five;
Had they been at their father's hand,
I had this night been man alive.
40.
'A farewell to my followers a',
And a' my neighbours gude at need;
Bid them think how the treacherous Ha's

Betrayed the life o' Parcy Reed.

41.

'The laird o' Clennel bears my bow,
The laird o' Brandon bears my brand;
Whene'er they ride i' the Border side,
They'll mind the fate o' the laird Troughend.'

BEWICK AND GRAHAME

THE TEXT is from several broadsides and chap-books, but mainly depends on a stall-copy entitled *The Song of Bewick and Grahame*, approximately dated 1740. Sir Walter Scott considered this ballad 'remarkable, as containing probably the very latest allusion to the institution of brotherhood in arms' (see 14.[4], and the use of the word 'bully'); but Child strongly suspects there was an older and better copy than those extant, none of which is earlier than the eighteenth century.

THE STORY is concerned with two fathers, who boast about their sons, and cause the two lads to fight. Christy Graham is faced with the dilemma of fighting either his father or his brother-in-arms, and decides to meet the latter; but, should he kill his friend, he determines not to return alive. Young Bewick takes a similar vow. They fight two hours, and at last an 'ackward' stroke kills Bewick, and Christy falls on his sword. The two fathers lament, and the ballad-singer finishes by putting the blame on them.

BEWICK AND GRAHAME

1.

OLD Grahame he is to Carlisle gone,
Where Sir Robert Bewick there met he;
In arms to the wine they are gone,
And drank till they were both merry.

2.

Old Grahame he took up the cup,
And said, 'Brother Bewick, here's to thee,
And here's to our two sons at home,
For they live best in our country.'

3.

'Nay, were thy son as good as mine,
And of some books he could but read,
With sword and buckler by his side,

To see how he could save his head.

4.

'They might have been call'd two bold brethren

Where ever they did go or ride;

They might have been call'd two bold brethren,

They might have crack'd the Border-side.

5.

5.² 'bully,' = billie, brother. See page 75.

Thy son is bad, and is but a lad,

And bully to my son cannot be;

For my son Bewick can both write and read,

And sure I am that cannot he.'

6.

'I put him to school, but he would not learn,

I bought him books but he would not read;

But my blessing he's never have

Till I see how his hand can save his head.'

7.

Old Grahame called for an account,

And he ask'd what was for to pay;

There he paid a crown, so it went round,

Which was all for good wine and hay.

8.

Old Grahame is into the stable gone,

Where stood thirty good steeds and three;

He's taken his own steed by the head,

And home rode he right wantonly.

9.

When he came home, there did he espy
A loving sight to spy or see,
There did he espy his own three sons,
Young Christy Grahame, the foremost was he.
10.
There did he espy his own three sons,
Young Christy Grahame, the foremost was he;
'Where have you been all day, father,
That no counsel you would take by me?'
11.
'Nay, I have been in Carlisle town,
Where Sir Robert Bewick there met me;
He said thou was bad, and call'd thee a lad,
And a baffled man by thou I be.
12.
'He said thou was bad, and call'd thee a lad,
And bully to his son cannot be;
For his son Bewick can both write and read,
And sure I am that cannot thee.

13.
'I put thee to school, but thou would not learn,
I bought thee books, but thou would not read;
But my blessing thou's never have
Till I see with Bewick thou can save thy head.'
14.
'Oh, pray forbear, my father dear;
That ever such a thing should be!
Shall I venture my body in field to fight

With a man that's faith and troth to me?'
15.
'What's that thou sayst, thou limmer loon?
Or how dare thou stand to speak to me?
If thou do not end this quarrel soon,
Here is my glove, thou shalt fight me.'
16.
Christy stoop'd low unto the ground,
Unto the ground, as you'll understand;
'O father, put on your glove again,
The wind hath blown it from your hand.'
17.
'What's that thou sayst, thou limmer loon?
Or how dare thou stand to speak to me?
If thou do not end this quarrel soon,
Here is my hand, thou shalt fight me.'
18.
Christy Grahame is to his chamber gone,
And for to study, as well might be,
Whether to fight with his father dear,
Or with his bully Bewick he.

19.
'If it be my fortune my bully to kill,
As you shall boldly understand,
In every town that I ride through,
They'll say, There rides a brotherless man!
20.
'Nay, for to kill my bully dear,

I think it will be a deadly sin;

And for to kill my father dear,

The blessing of heaven I ne'er shall win.

21.

'O give me your blessing, father,' he said,

'And pray well for me for to thrive;

If it be my fortune my bully to kill,

I swear I'll ne'er come home alive.'

22.

He put on his back a good plate-jack,

And on his head a cap of steel,

With sword and buckler by his side;

O gin he did not become them well!

23.

'O fare thee well, my father dear!

And fare thee well, thou Carlisle town!

If it be my fortune my bully to kill,

I swear I'll ne'er eat bread again.'

24.

24.[2] 'belive,' soon.

Now we'll leave talking of Christy Grahame,

And talk of him again belive;

But we will talk of bonny Bewick,

Where he was teaching his scholars five.

25.

Now when he had learn'd them well to fence,

To handle their swords without any doubt,

He's taken his own sword under his arm,

And walk'd his father's close about.

26.

26.² 'farleys,' wonders, novelties.

He look'd between him and the sun,

To see what farleys he could see;

There he spy'd a man with armour on,

As he came riding over the lee.

27.

'I wonder much what man yon be

That so boldly this way does come;

I think it is my nighest friend,

I think it is my bully Grahame.

28.

'O welcome, O welcome, bully Grahame!

O man, thou art my dear, welcome!

O man, thou art my dear, welcome!

For I love thee best in Christendom.'

29.

'Away, away, O bully Bewick,

And of thy bullyship let me be!

The day is come I never thought on;

Bully, I'm come here to fight with thee.'

30.

'O no! not so, O bully Grahame!

That e'er such a word should spoken be!

I was thy master, thou was my scholar;

So well as I have learned thee.'

31.

'My father he was in Carlisle town,
Where thy father Bewick there met he;
He said I was bad, and he call'd me a lad,
And a baffled man by thou I be.'
32.
'Away, away, O bully Grahame,
And of all that talk, man, let us be!
We'll take three men of either side
To see if we can our fathers agree.'
33.
'Away, away, O bully Bewick,
And of thy bullyship let me be!
But if thou be a man, as I trow thou art,
Come over this ditch and fight with me.'
34.
'O no, not so, my bully Grahame!
That e'er such a word should spoken be!
Shall I venture my body in field to fight
With a man that's faith and troth to me?'
35.
'Away, away, O bully Bewick,
And of all that care, man, let us be!
If thou be a man, as I trow thou art,
Come over this ditch and fight with me.'
36.
'Now, if it be my fortune thee, Grahame, to kill,
As God's will's, man, it all must be:
But if it be my fortune thee, Grahame, to kill,
'Tis home again I'll never gae.'

37.

'Thou art then of my mind, bully Bewick,

And sworn-brethren will we be;

If thou be a man, as I trow thou art,

Come over this ditch and fight with me.'

38.

He flang his cloak from off his shoulders,

His psalm-book out of his hand flung he,

He clap'd his hand upon the hedge,

And o'er lap he right wantonly.

39.

When Grahame did see his bully come,

The salt tear stood long in his eye;

'Now needs must I say that thou art a man,

That dare venture thy body to fight with me.

40.

'Now I have a harness on my back;

I know that thou hath none on thine;

But as little as thou hath on thy back,

Sure as little shall there be on mine.'

41.

He flang his jack from off his back,

His steel cap from his head flang he;

He's taken his sword into his hand,

He's tyed his horse unto a tree.

42.

Now they fell to it with two broad swords,

For two long hours fought Bewick and he;

Much sweat was to be seen on them both,
But never a drop of blood to see.

43.
Now Grahame gave Bewick an ackward stroke,
An ackward stroke surely struck he;
He struck him now under the left breast,
Then down to the ground as dead fell he.

44.
'Arise, arise, O bully Bewick,
Arise, and speak three words to me!
Whether this be thy deadly wound,
Or God and good surgeons will mend thee.'

45.
'O horse, O horse, O bully Grahame,
And pray do get thee far from me!
Thy sword is sharp, it hath wounded my heart,
And so no further can I gae.

46.
'O horse, O horse, O bully Grahame,
And get thee far from me with speed!
And get thee out of this country quite!
That none may know who's done the deed.'

47.
'O if this be true, my bully dear,
The words that thou dost tell to me,
The vow I made, and the vow I'll keep;
I swear I'll be the first to die.'

48.

48.[1] 'moudie-hill,' mole-hill.

Then he stuck his sword in a moudie-hill,

Where he lap thirty good foot and three;

First he bequeathed his soul to God,

And upon his own sword-point lap he.

49.

Now Grahame he was the first that died,

And then came Robin Bewick to see;

'Arise, arise, O son,' he said,

'For I see thou's won the victory.

50.

'Arise, arise, O son,' he said,

'For I see thou's won the victory;'

'Father, could ye not drunk your wine at home,

And letten me and my brother be?

51.

'Nay, dig a grave both low and wide,

And in it us two pray bury;

But bury my bully Grahame on the sun-side,

For I'm sure he's won the victory.'

52.

Now we'll leave talking of these two brethren,

In Carlisle town where they lie slain,

And talk of these two good old men,

Where they were making a pitiful moan.

53.

With that bespoke now Robin Bewick;

'O man, was I not much to blame?

I have lost one of the liveliest lads

That ever was bred unto my name.'

54.

With that bespoke my good lord Grahame;

'O man, I have lost the better block;

I have lost my comfort and my joy,

I have lost my key, I have lost my lock.

55.

'Had I gone through all Ladderdale,

And forty horse had set on me,

Had Christy Grahame been at my back,

So well as he would guarded me.'

56.

I have no more of my song to sing,

But two or three words to you I'll name;

But 'twill be talk'd in Carlisle town

That these two old men were all the blame.

THE FIRE OF FRENDRAUGHT

THE TEXT is from Motherwell's *Minstrelsy*. He received the ballad from Charles Kirkpatrick Sharp. In Maidment's *North Countrie Garland* there is a similar version with a number of small verbal differences.

THE STORY.—Frendraught in Aberdeenshire, and Rothiemay in Banffshire, lie on opposite sides of the Deveron, which separates the counties. A feud began (as the result of a dispute over fishing rights) between Crichton of Frendraught and Gordon of Rothiemay, and in a fight on the first day of the year 1630, Rothiemay and others were killed. Kinsmen of both parties were involved; and though the broil was temporarily settled, another soon sprang up. The Lord John of the ballad was Viscount Melgum, the second son of the Marquis of Huntly, who was appealed to as a peacemaker between the factions of Leslie and Crichton. Lord John and Rothiemay were sent by the Marquis to escort Frendraught to his home, a precaution rendered necessary by the knowledge that the Leslies were in ambuscade. Arrived at Frendraught, the laird and lady entreated the two young men to remain the night, and eventually prevailed on them to do so.

However (though it was long disputed whether the fire was an accident or not), it seems that the ancient grudge against Rothiemay moved Frendraught to sacrifice 'a great quantity of silver, both coined and uncoined,' in the firing of his house for the sake of burning Rothiemay.

Sophia Hay (25.[1]) was the daughter of the Earl of Erroll, and Viscount Melgum's wife. The last two lines of the ballad are not easily explained, as the lady is recorded to have been deeply attached to her husband; but it is possible that they have been inserted from a similar stanza in some other ballad.

THE FIRE OF FRENDRAUGHT

1.

THE eighteenth of October,

A dismal tale to hear

How good Lord John and Rothiemay

Was both burnt in the fire.

2.

When steeds was saddled and well bridled,

And ready for to ride,
Then out it came her false Frendraught,
Inviting them to bide.

3.
Said, 'Stay this night untill we sup,
The morn untill we dine;
'Twill be a token of good 'greement
'Twixt your good Lord and mine.'

4.
'We'll turn again,' said good Lord John;
'But no,' said Rothiemay,
'My steed's trapan'd, my bridle's broken,
I fear the day I'm fey.'

5.
When mass was sung, and bells was rung,
And all men bound for bed,
Then good Lord John and Rothiemay
In one chamber was laid.

6.
They had not long cast off their cloaths,
And were but now asleep,
When the weary smoke began to rise,
Likewise the scorching heat.

7.
'O waken, waken, Rothiemay!
O waken, brother dear!
And turn you to our Saviour;
There is strong treason here.'

8.

When they were dressed in their cloaths,
And ready for to boun,
The doors and windows was all secured,
The roof-tree burning down.

9.

He did him to the wire-window
As fast as he could gang;
Says 'Wae to the hands put in the stancheons!
For out we'll never win.'

10.

When he stood at the wire-window,
Most doleful to be seen,
He did espy her Lady Frendraught,
Who stood upon the green.

11.

Cried 'Mercy, mercy, Lady Frendraught,
Will ye not sink with sin?
For first your husband killed my father,
And now you burn his son.'

12.

O then out spoke her Lady Frendraught,
And loudly did she cry;
'It were great pity for good Lord John,
But none for Rothiemay;
But the keys are casten in the deep draw well,
Ye cannot get away.'

13.

While he stood in this dreadful plight,
Most piteous to be seen,
There called out his servant Gordon,
As he had frantic been.

14.

'O loup, O loup, my dear master!
O loup and come to me!
I'll catch you in my arms two,
One foot I will not flee.

15.

'O loup, O loup, my dear master!
O loup and come away!
I'll catch you in my arms two,
But Rothiemay may lie.'

16.

16.4 'twin,' part.

'The fish shall never swim in the flood,
Nor corn grow through the clay,
Nor the fiercest fire that was ever kindled
Twin me and Rothiemay.

17.

'But I cannot loup, I cannot come,
I cannot win to thee;
My head's fast in the wire-window,
My feet burning from me.

18.

'My eyes are seething in my head,
My flesh roasting also,

My bowels are boiling with my blood;

Is not that a woeful woe?

19.

'Take here the rings from my white fingers,

That are so long and small,

And give them to my lady fair,

Where she sits in her hall.

20.

'So I cannot loup, I cannot come,

I cannot loup to thee;

My earthly part is all consumed,

My spirit but speaks to thee.'

21.

Wringing her hands, tearing her hair,

His lady she was seen,

And thus addressed his servant Gordon,

Where he stood on the green.

22.

'O wae be to you, George Gordon!

An ill death may you die!

So safe and sound as you stand there

And my lord bereaved from me.'

23.

'I bad him loup, I bad him come,

I bad him loup to me;

I'd catch him in my arms two,

A foot I should not flee.

24.

'He threw me the rings from his white fingers,

Which were so long and small,

To give to you, his lady fair,

Where you sat in your hall.'

25.

Sophia Hay, Sophia Hay,

O bonny Sophia was her name,

Her waiting-maid put on her cloaths,

But I wot she tore them off again.

26.

And aft she cried, 'Ohon! alas! alas!

A sair heart's ill to win;

I wan a sair heart when I married him,

And the day it's well return'd again.'

GEORDIE

THE TEXT is from Johnson's *Museum*, communicated by Robert Burns.

THE STORY.—Some editors have identified the hero of the ballad with George Gordon, fourth earl of Huntly, but upon what grounds it is difficult to see.

There are two English broadside ballads, of the first and second halves respectively of the seventeenth century, which are either the originals of, or copies from, the Scottish ballad, which exists in many variants. The earlier is concerned with 'the death of a worthy gentleman named George Stoole,' 'to a delicate Scottish tune,' and the second is called 'The Life and Death of George of Oxford. To a pleasant tune, called Poor Georgy.' One of the Scottish versions has a burden resembling that of 'George Stoole.'

The 'battle in the north' and Sir Charles Hay are not identified.

GEORDIE

1.

1.4 'wyte,' blame.

THERE was a battle in the north,

And nobles there was many,

And they hae killed Sir Charlie Hay,

And they laid the wyte on Geordie.

2.

O he has written a lang letter,

He sent it to his lady:

'Ye maun cum up to Enbrugh town,

To see what word's o' Geordie.'

3.

3.4 'wallowt,' drooped.

When first she look'd the letter on,

She was both red and rosy;

But she had na read a word but twa
Till she wallowt like a lily.

4.

4.² 'menyie,' attendants.

'Gar get to me ray gude grey steed;
My menyie a' gae wi' me;
For I shall neither eat nor drink
Till Enbrugh town shall see me.'

5.

And she has mountit her gude grey steed,
Her menyie a' gaed wi' her,
And she did neither eat nor drink
Till Enbrugh town did see her,

6.

And first appear'd the fatal block,
And syne the aix to head him,
And Geordie cumin' down the stair,
And bands o' airn upon him.

7.

But tho' he was chain'd in fetters strang,
O' airn and steel sae heavy,
There was na ane in a' the court
Sae bra' a man as Geordie.

8.

O she's down on her bended knee;
I wat she's pale and weary:
'O pardon, pardon, noble king,
And gie me back my dearie!

9.

'I hae born seven sons to my Geordie dear,

The seventh ne'er saw his daddie,

O pardon, pardon, noble king,

Pity a waefu' lady!'

10.

'Gar bid the headin'-man mak haste,'

Our king reply'd fu' lordly:

'O noble king, tak a' that's mine,

But gie me back my Geordie!'

11.

The Gordons cam, the Gordons ran,

And they were stark and steady,

And ay the word amang them a'

Was 'Gordons, keep you ready!'

12.

An aged lord at the king's right hand

Says 'Noble king, but hear me;

Gar her tell down five thousand pound,

And gie her back her dearie.'

13.

Some gae her marks, some gae her crowns,

Some gae her dollars many,

And she's tell'd down five thousand pound,

And she's gotten again her dearie.

14.

14.³ 'bouk,' body.

14.⁴ 'Or,' ere; 'tint,' lost.

She blinkit blythe in her Geordie's face,

- 125 -

Says 'Dear I've bought thee, Geordie;
But there sud been bluidy bouks on the green
Or I had tint my laddie.'

15.
He claspit her by the middle sma',
And he kist her lips sae rosy:
'The fairest flower o' woman-kind
Is my sweet bonnie lady!'

THE BARON OF BRACKLEY

THE TEXT is from Alexander Laing's *Scarce Ancient Ballads* (1822). A similar version occurs in Buchan's *Gleanings* (1825). Professor Gummere, in printing the first text, omits six stanzas, on the assumption that they represent part of a second ballad imperfectly incorporated. But I think the ballad can be read as it stands below, though doubtless 'his ladie's' remark, st. 11, is out of place.

THE STORY seems to be a combination of at least two. An old Baron of Brackley, 'an honest aged man,' was slain in 1592 by 'caterans' or freebooters who had been entertained hospitably by him. In 1666 John Gordon of Brackley began a feud with John Farquharson of Inverey by seizing some cattle or horses—accounts differ—by way of fines due for taking fish out of season. This eventually led to the slaying of Brackley and certain of his adherents.

Professor Child suspects a commixture of the two episodes in the one ballad, or more probably, a grafting of a later ballad on to an earlier one. The character of the Baron as revealed in the ballad more closely resembles that of the 1592 episode, while the details of the fray are in keeping with the later story.

'Peggy,' the Baron's wife, was Margaret Burnet, cousin to Gilbert, Bishop of Salisbury. After Brackley's death she married again, but not her husband's murderer, as the end of our ballad scandalously suggests.

Brackley is near Ballater, about forty miles west of Aberdeen.

THE BARON OF BRACKLEY

1.

1.² 'yett,' gate.

INVEREY cam doun Deeside, whistlin' and playin',

He was at brave Braikley's yett ere it was dawin'.

2.

He rappit fu' loudly an' wi' a great roar,

Cried, 'Cum doun, cum doun, Braikley, and open the door.

3.

'Are ye sleepin', Baronne, or are ye wakin'?
Ther's sharpe swords at your yett, will gar your blood spin.

4.

'Open the yett, Braikley, and lat us within,
Till we on the green turf gar your bluid rin.'

5.

5.² 'spulyie,' spoil.

Out spak the brave baronne, owre the castell-wa';
'Are ye cum to spulyie and plunder mi ha'?

6.

'But gin ye be gentlemen, licht and cum in:
Gin ye drink o' my wine, ye'll nae gar my bluid spin.

7.

7.¹ 'widifu's,' gallows-birds (lit. 'halter-fulls').

'Gin ye be hir'd widifu's, ye may gang by,
Ye may gang to the lowlands and steal their fat ky.

8.

8.¹ 'rievers,' robbers; 'ketterin' = cateran, marauder freebooter.

'Ther spulyie like rievers o' wyld ketterin clan,
Who plunder unsparing baith houses and lan'.

9.

'Gin ye be gentlemen, licht and cum [in],
Ther's meat and drink i' my ha' for every man.

10.

'Gin ye be hired widifu's, ye may gang by,
Gang doun to the lowlands, and steal horse and ky.'

11.

Up spak his ladie, at his bak where she lay,

- 128 -

'Get up, get up, Braikley, an be not afraid;

The'r but young hir'd widifu's wi' belted plaids.'

12.

'Cum kiss me, mi Peggy, I'le nae langer stay,

For I will go out and meet Inverey.

13.

'But haud your tongue, Peggy, and mak nae sic din,

For yon same hir'd widifu's will prove themselves men.'

14.

14.² 'rocks,' distaffs.

She called on her marys, they cam to her hand;

Cries, 'Bring me your rocks, lassies, we will them command.

15.

'Get up, get up, Braikley, and turn bak your ky,

Or me and mi women will them defy.

16.

'Cum forth then, mi maidens, and show them some play;

We'll ficht them, and shortly the cowards will fly.

17.

'Gin I had a husband, whereas I hae nane,

He woud nae ly i' his bed and see his ky taen.

18.

'Ther's four-and-twenty milk-whit calves, twal o' them ky,

In the woods o' Glentanner, it's ther thei a' ly.

19.

'Ther's goat i' the Etnach, and sheep o' the brae,

An a' will be plunder'd by young Inverey.'

20.

'Now haud your tongue, Peggy, and gie me a gun,
Ye'll see me gae furth, but I'll never cum in.
21.
'Call mi brother William, mi unkl also,
Mi cousin James Gordon; we'll mount and we'll go.'
22.
When Braikley was ready and stood i' the closs,
He was the bravest baronne that e'er mounted horse.

23.
Whan all wer assembled o' the castell green,
No man like brave Braikley was ther to be seen.
24.
    .   .   .   .   .
'Turn bak, brother William, ye are a bridegroom;
25.
'Wi' bonnie Jean Gordon, the maid o' the mill;
O' sichin' and sobbin' she'll soon get her fill.'
26.
'I'm no coward, brother, 'tis ken'd I'm a man;
I'll ficht i' your quarral as lang's I can stand.
27.
'I'll ficht, my dear brother, wi' heart and gudewill,
And so will young Harry that lives at the mill.
28.
'But turn, mi dear brother, and nae langer stay:
What'll cum o' your ladie, gin Braikley thei slay?
29.
'What'll cum o' your ladie and bonnie young son?

O what'll cum o' them when Braikley is gone?'
30.
'I never will turn: do you think I will fly?
But here I will ficht, and here I will die.'

31.
'Strik, dogs,' crys Inverey, 'and ficht till ye're slayn,
For we are four hundred, ye are but four men.
32.
'Strik, strik, ye proud boaster, your honour is gone,
Your lands we will plunder, your castell we'll burn.'
33.
At the head o' the Etnach the battel began,
At Little Auchoilzie thei kill'd the first man.
34.
First thei kill'd ane, and soon they kill'd twa,
Thei kill'd gallant Braikley, the flour o' them a'.
35.
Thei kill'd William Gordon, and James o' the Knox,
And brave Alexander, the flour o' Glenmuick.
36.
What sichin' and moaning was heard i' the glen,
For the Baronne o' Braikley, who basely was slayn!
37.
'Cam ye bi the castell, and was ye in there?
Saw ye pretty Peggy tearing her hair?'
38.
'Yes, I cam by Braikley, and I gaed in there,
And there saw his ladie braiding her hair.

39.

'She was rantin', and dancin', and singin' for joy,

And vowin' that nicht she woud feest Inverey.

40.

'She eat wi' him, drank wi' him, welcom'd him in,

Was kind to the man that had slain her baronne.'

41.

Up spake the son on the nourice's knee,

'Gin I live to be a man, revenged I'll be.'

42.

Ther's dool i' the kitchin, and mirth i' the ha',

The Baronne o' Braikley is dead and awa'.

THE GIPSY LADDIE

THE TEXT is from Motherwell's MS., a copy from tradition in Renfrewshire in 1825. The ballad exists both in English and Scottish, and though the English ballad is probably derived from the Scottish, it was the first in print. It is also called *Johnnie Faa*. Motherwell, in printing an elaborated version of the following text (*Minstrelsy*, 1827, p. 360), called it *Gypsie Davy*.

THE STORY.—Singers—presumably gipsies—entice Lady Cassillis down to hear them, and cast glamour on her. She follows their chief, Gipsy Davy, but finds (stt. 5 and 6) that the conditions are changed. Her lord misses her, seeks her 'thro' nations many,' and finds her drinking with the gipsy chief. He asks her to return home with him. At this point the present version becomes difficult, and the bearing of st. 12 is not apparent. We may gather that the lady returned home with her husband, as he proceeded to hang sixteen of the gipsies.

This version calls the lady 'Jeanie Faw,' but the majority call the gipsy chief Johnnie Faa, which is a well-known name amongst gipsies, and occurs as early as 1540 as the name of the 'lord and earl of Little Egypt.' Gipsies being expelled from Scotland by Act of Parliament in 1609, a Captain Johnnë Faa and seven others were hanged in 1624 for disobeying the ordinance, and this execution is sufficient to account for the introduction of the name into a ballad of this kind.

The ballad has no certain connection with the Cassillis family, and it has been suggested that the word is simply a corruption of 'castle,' the original beginning of the ballad being

> 'The gipsies came to the castle-gate.'

If this be so, the present form of the ballad illustrates admirably two methods of corruption by tradition.

THE GIPSY LADDIE

1.
THERE cam singers to Earl Cassillis' gates,
And oh, but they sang bonnie!
They sang sae sweet and sae complete,
Till down cam the earl's lady.

2.

2.³ 'weel-faur'd,' well-favoured.

She cam tripping down the stair,
And all her maids before her;
As soon as they saw her weel-faur'd face
They coost their glamourye owre her.

3.

They gave her o' the gude sweet-meats,
The nutmeg and the ginger,
And she gied them a far better thing,
Ten gold rings aff her finger.

4.

'Tak from me my silken cloak,
And bring me down my plaidie;
For it is good eneuch,' she said,
'To follow a Gipsy Davy.

5.

5.⁴ 'a wheen,' a pack [of].

'Yestreen I rode this water deep,
And my gude lord beside me;
But this nicht I maun set in my pretty fit and wade,
A wheen blackguards wading wi' me,

6.

'Yestreen I lay in a fine feather-bed,
And my gude lord beyond me;
But this nicht I maun lie in some cauld tenant's-barn,
A wheen blackguards waiting on me.'

7.

'Come to thy bed, my bonny Jeanie Faw,
Come to thy bed, my dearie,
For I do swear by the top o' my spear,
Thy gude lord'll nae mair come near thee.'

8.
When her gude lord cam hame at nicht,
It was asking for his fair ladye;
One spak slow, and another whisper'd out,
'She's awa' wi' Gipsey Davy!'

9.
'Come saddle to me my horse,' he said;
'Come saddle and mak him readie!
For I'll neither sleep, eat, nor drink,
Till I find out my lady.'

10.
They socht her up, they socht her doun,
They socht her thro' nations many,
Till at length they found her out in Abbey dale,
Drinking wi' Gipsey Davy.

11.
'Rise, oh, rise! my bonny Jeanie Faw;
Oh, rise, and do not tarry!
Is this the thing ye promised to me
When at first I did thee marry?'

12.
They drank her cloak, so did they her goun,
They drank her stockings and her shoon,
And they drank the coat that was nigh to her smock,

And they pawned her pearled apron.

13.

They were sixteen clever men,

Suppose they were na bonnie;

They are a' to be hang'd on ae tree,

For the stealing o' Earl Cassilis' lady.

14.

'We are sixteen clever men,

One woman was a' our mother;

We are a' to be hanged on ae day,

For the stealing of a wanton lady.'

BESSY BELL AND MARY GRAY

THE TEXT is from Sharpe's *Ballad Book*. A parody of this ballad, concerning an episode of the end of the seventeenth century, shows it to have been popular not long after its making. In England it has become a nursery rhyme (see Halliwell's *Nursery Rhymes*, p. 246).

THE STORY.—In 1781 a Major Barry, then owner of Lednock, recorded the following tradition. Mary Gray was the daughter of the Laird of Lednock, near Perth, and Bessy Bell was the daughter of the Laird of Kinvaid, a neighbouring place. Both were handsome, and the two were intimate friends. Bessy Bell being come on a visit to Mary Gray, they retired, in order to avoid an outbreak of the plague, to a bower built by themselves in a romantic spot called Burnbraes, on the side of Branchieburn, three-quarters of a mile from Lednock House. The ballad does not say *how* the 'pest cam,' but tradition finds a cause for their deaths by inventing a young man, in love with both, who visited them and brought the infection. They died in the bower, and were buried in the Dranochhaugh ('Stronach haugh,' 3.[3]), near the bank of the river Almond. The grave is still visited by pious pilgrims.

Major Barry mentions 1666 as the year, but the plague did not reach Scotland in that year. Probably the year in question was 1645, when the district was ravaged with the pestilence.

BESSY BELL AND MARY GRAY

1.

1.[3] 'bigget,' built.

1.[4] 'theekit,' thatched.

O BESSIE Bell and Mary Gray,
They war twa bonnie lasses;
They bigget a bower on yon burn-brae,
And theekit it o'er wi' rashes.

2.

They theekit it o'er wi' rashes green,
They theekit it o'er wi' heather;

But the pest cam frae the burrows-town,
And slew them baith thegither.

3.

3.[4] *i.e.* to bask beneath the sun.

They thought to lie in Methven kirk-yard,
Amang their noble kin;
But they maun lye in Stronach haugh,
To biek forenent the sin.

4.

And Bessy Bell and Mary Gray,
They war twa bonnie lasses;
They bigget a bower on yon burn-brae,
And theekit it o'er wi' rashes.

SIR JAMES THE ROSE

THE TEXT is from Motherwell's *Minstrelsy* (1827). It is based on a stall-copy, presumably similar to one preserved by Sir Walter Scott at Abbotsford, combined with a version from recitation, which Child none the less calls 'well remembered from print.'

THE STORY has no historical foundation, as far as can be discovered; and for once we have a traditional tale inculcating a moral, though we do not understand why the 'nourice' betrays Sir James to his enemies.

Michael Bruce wrote a version of the story of this ballad, which seems to have become more popular than the ballad itself. It may be seen in A. B. Grosart's edition of his works (1865), p. 197.

SIR JAMES THE ROSE

1.

O HEARD ye of Sir James the Rose,

The young heir of Buleighan?

For he has killed a gallant squire,

And his friends are out to take him.

2.

Now he's gone to the house of Marr,

Where the Nourice was his leman;

To seek his dear he did repair,

Thinking she would befriend him.

3.

'Where are you going, Sir James?' she says,

'Or where now are you riding?'

'Oh, I am bound to a foreign land,

For now I'm under hiding.

4.

'Where shall I go? where shall I run?

Where shall I go to hide me?
For I have killed a gallant squire,
And they're seeking to slay me.'
5.
'O go ye down to yon ale-house,
And I'll there pay your lawin';
And if I be a maiden true,
I'll meet you in the dawin'.'
6.
'I'll no go down to yon ale-house,
For you to pay my lawin';
There's forty shillings for one supper,
I'll stay in't till the dawin'.'
7.
7.² 'brechan,' plaid.
He's turned him richt and round about,
And rowed him in his brechan;
And he has gone to take his sleep,
In the lowlands of Buleighan.
8.
He had not weel gone out o' sicht,
Nor was he past Millstrethen,
Till four-and-twenty belted knights,
Came riding owre the Lethan.

9.
'O have ye seen Sir James the Rose,
The young heir of Buleighan?
For he has killed a gallant squire,

And we're sent out to take him.'

10.

'O I have seen Sir James,' she says,

'For he passed here on Monday;

If the steed be swift that he rides on,

He's past the gates o' London.'

11.

As they rode on man after man,

Then she cried out behind them,

'If you do seek Sir James the Rose,

I'll tell you where you'll find him.'

12.

'Seek ye the bank abune the mill,

In the lowlands of Buleighan;

And there you'll find Sir James the Rose,

Lying sleeping in his brechan.

13.

'You must not wake him out of sleep,

Nor yet must you affright him,

Till you drive a dart quite through his heart,

And through his body pierce him.'

14.

They sought the bank abune the mill,

In the lowlands of Buleighan,

And there they found Sir James the Rose,

Lying sleeping in his brechan.

15.

Up then spake Sir John the Graeme

Who had the charge a-keeping,

'It shall ne'er be said, dear gentlemen,
We killed a man when a-sleeping.'

16.
They seized his broad sword and his targe,
And closely him surrounded;
And when he waked out of his sleep,
His senses were confounded.

17.
'O pardon, pardon, gentlemen,
Have mercy now upon me.'
'Such as you gave, such you shall have,
And so we fall upon thee.'

18.
'Donald, my man, wait me upon,
And I'll gie you my brechan;
And if you stay here till I die,
You'll get my trews of tartan.

19.
'There is fifty pounds in my pocket,
Besides my trews and brechan,
Ye'll get my watch and diamond ring,
And take me to Loch-Largan.'

20.
Now they've ta'en out his bleeding heart,
And stuck it on a spear,
Then took it to the House of Marr,
And gave it to his dear.

21.

But when she saw his bleeding heart,
She was like one distracted,
She wrung her hands and tore her hair,
Crying, 'Oh! what have I acted.
22.
'It's for your sake, Sir James the Rose,
That my poor heart's a-breaking;
Cursed be the day I did thee betray,
Thou brave knight o' Buleighan.'

23.
Then up she rose, and forth she goes,
And in that fatal hour
She bodily was borne away,
And never was seen more.
24.
But where she went was never kent;
And so, to end the matter,
A traitor's end you may depend
Can never be no better.

CLYDE'S WATER

THE TEXT is from the Skene MS., but I have omitted the three final lines, which do not make a complete stanza, and, when compared with Scott's 'Old Lady's' version, are obviously corrupt. The last verse should signify that the mothers of Willie and Meggie went up and down the bank saying, 'Clyde's water has done us wrong!'

The ballad is better known as *Willie and May Margaret*.

THE STORY.—Willie refuses his mother's request to stay at home, as he wishes to visit his true-love. The mother puts her malison, or curse, upon him, but he rides off. Clyde is roaring, but Willie says, 'Drown me as I come back, but spare me as I go,' which is Martial's

'Parcite dum propero, mergite cum redeo,'

and occurs in other English broadsides. Meggie will not admit Willie, and he rides away. Meggie awakes, and learns that she has dismissed her true-love in her sleep. Our ballad is deficient here, but it is obvious from st. 19 that both lovers are drowned. We must understand, therefore, that Meggie follows Willie across Clyde. A variant of the ballad explains that she found him 'in the deepest pot' in all Clyde's water, and drowned herself.

Child notes that there is a very popular Italian ballad of much the same story, except that the mother's curse is on the girl and not the man.

There is a curious change in the style of spelling from stanza 15 to the end.

CLYDE'S WATER

1.

'YE gie corn unto my horse,

An' meat unto my man,

For I will gae to my true-love's gates

This night, gin that I can.'

2.

'O stay at hame this ae night, Willie,

This ae bare night wi' me;

The best bed in a' my house

Sall be well made to thee.'

3.

'I carena for your beds, mither,

I carena ae pin,

For I'll gae to my love's gates

This night, gin I can win.'

4.

'O stay, my son Willie, this night,

This ae night wi' me;

The best hen in a' my roost

Sall be well made ready for thee.'

5.

'I carena for your hens, mither,

I carena ae pin;

I sall gae to my love's gates

This night, gin I can win.'

6.

6.4 'malisen,' curse.

'Gin ye winna stay, my son Willie,

This ae bare night wi' me,

Gin Clyde's water be deep and fu' o' flood,

My malisen drown ye!'

7.

7.4 'fleyt,' frightened.

He rode up yon high hill,

An' down yon dowie glen;

The roaring o' Clyde's water

Wad hae fleyt ten thousand men.

8.

'O spare me, Clyde's water,

O spare me as I gae!

Mak me your wrack as I come back,

But spare me as I gae!'

9.

He rade in, and farther in,

Till he came to the chin;

And he rade in, and farther in,

Till he came to dry lan'.

10.

And whan he came to his love's gates,

He tirled at the pin.

'Open your gates, Meggie,

Open your gates to me,

For my beets are fu' o' Clyde's water,

And the rain rains oure my chin.'

11.

'I hae nae lovers therout,' she says,

'I hae nae love within;

My true-love is in my arms twa,

An' nane will I lat in.'

12.

'Open your gates, Meggie, this ae night,

Open your gates to me;

For Clyde's water is fu' o' flood,

An' my mither's malison'll drown me.'

13.

'Ane o' my chamers is fu' o' corn,' she says,

'An' ane is fu' o' hay;
Anither is fu' o' gentlemen,
An' they winna move till day.'
14.
14.⁴ 'read,' interpret.
14.⁶ 'standing,' *staring* in manuscript.
Out waked her May Meggie,
Out o' her drousy dream:
'I dreamed a dream sin the yestreen,
(God read a' dreams to guid!)
That my true-love Willie
Was standing at my bed-feet.'
15.
'Now lay ye still, my ae dochter,
An' keep my back fra the call',
For it's na the space of hafe an hour
Sen he gad fra yer hall'.'
16.
'An' hey, Willie, an' hoa, Willie,
Winne ye turn agen?'
But ay the louder that she crayed
He rod agenst the wind.
17.
He rod up yon high hill,
An' doun yon douey den;
The roring that was in Clide's water
Wad ha' flayed ten thousand men.

18.

He road in, an' farder in,
Till he came to the chine;
An' he road in, an' farder in,
Bat never mare was seen.

.   .   .   .   .

19.

19.[4] 'sneed,' snood, fillet.

Ther was na mare seen of that guid lord
Bat his hat frae his head;
There was na mare seen of that lady
Bat her comb an' her sneed.

.   .   .   .   .

KATHARINE JAFFRAY

THE TEXT is from Herd's MSS., two copies showing a difference of one word and a few spellings. Stt. 3 and 5 are interchanged for the sake of the sense.

Many copies of this ballad exist (Child prints a dozen), but this one is both the shortest and simplest.

THE STORY.—In *The Cruel Brother* (First Series, p. 76) it was shown that a lover must 'speak to the brother' of his lady. Here the lesson, it seems, is that he must 'tell the lass herself' before her wedding-day. Katharine, however, not only proves her faith to her first lover (her 'grass-green' dress, 10.², shows an ill-omened marriage), but prefers the Scot to the Southron. This lesson the ballad drives home in the last two verses.

Presumably Scott founded *Young Lochinvar* on the story of this ballad, as in six versions the Scots laird bears that name.

KATHARINE JAFFRAY

1.

THERE liv'd a lass in yonder dale,

And doun in yonder glen, O,

And Kath'rine Jaffray was her name,

Well known by many men, O.

2.

Out came the Laird of Lauderdale,

Out frae the South Countrie,

All for to court this pretty maid,

Her bridegroom for to be.

3.

He has teld her father and mither baith,

And a' the rest o' her kin,

And has teld the lass hersell,

And her consent has win.

4.

Then came the Laird of Lochinton,
Out frae the English border,
All for to court this pretty maid,
Well mounted in good order.

5.

He's teld her father and mither baith,
As I hear sindry say,
But he has nae teld the lass hersell,
Till on her wedding day.

6.

When day was set, and friends were met,
And married to be,
Lord Lauderdale came to the place,
The bridal for to see.

7.

'O are you come for sport, young man?
Or are you come for play?
Or are you come for a sight o' our bride,
Just on her wedding day?'

8.

'I'm nouther come for sport,' he says,
'Nor am I come for play;
But if I had one sight o' your bride,
I'll mount and ride away.'

9.

There was a glass of the red wine
Fill'd up them atween,

And ay she drank to Lauderdale,

Wha her true-love had been.

10.

Then he took her by the milk-white hand,

And by the grass-green sleeve,

And he mounted her high behind him there,

At the bridegroom he askt nae leive.

11.

Then the blude run down by Cowden Banks,

And down by Cowden Braes,

And ay she gard the trumpet sound,

'O this is foul, foul play!'

12.

Now a' ye that in England are,

Or are in England born,

Come nere to Scotland to court a lass,

Or else ye'l get the scorn.

13.

13.[1] 'haik ye up,' kidnap (*Jamieson*), but ? delude, or keep in suspense.

They haik ye up and settle ye by,

Till on your wedding day,

And gie ye frogs instead o' fish,

And play ye foul, foul play.

LIZIE LINDSAY

THE TEXT is from Kinloch's MSS. He obtained it from Mearnsshire, and remarks that according to the tradition of that district the heroine was said to have been a daughter of Lindsay of Edzell, though he had searched in vain for genealogical confirmation of the tradition.

THE STORY.—'Ballads of this description,' says Professor Child, 'are peculiarly liable to interpolation and debasement.' In this version the most offending stanza is the tenth; and the extra two lines in stt. 22 and 24 also appear to be unnecessary. The anapaestic metre of this version should be noted.

The ballad was and is a great favourite with singers, and the tune may be found in several of the collections of Scottish songs.

LIZIE LINDSAY

1.

IT's of a young lord o' the Hielands,

A bonnie braw castle had he,

And he says to his lady mither,

'My boon ye will grant to me:

Sall I gae to Edinbruch city,

And fesh hame a lady wi' me?'

2.

'Ye may gae to Edinbruch city,

And fesh hame a lady wi' thee,

But see that ye bring her but flatt'rie,

And court her in grit povertie.'

3.

'My coat, mither, sall be o' the plaiden,

A tartan kilt oure my knee,

Wi' hosens and brogues and the bonnet;

I'll court her wi' nae flatt'rie.'

4.

Whan he cam to Edinbruch city,
He play'd at the ring and the ba',
And saw monie a bonnie young ladie,
But Lizie Lindsay was first o' them a'.

5.

Syne, dress'd in his Hieland grey plaiden,
His bonnet abune his e'e-bree,
He called on fair Lizie Lindsay;
Says, 'Lizie, will ye fancy me?

6.

'And gae to the Hielands, my lassie,
And gae, gae wi' me?
O gae to the Hielands, Lizie Lindsay,
I'll feed ye on curds and green whey.

7.

'And ye'se get a bed o' green bracken;
My plaidie will hap thee and me;
Ye'se lie in my arms, bonnie Lizie,
If ye'll gae to the Hielands wi' me.'

8.

'O how can I gae to the Hielands
Or how can I gae wi' thee,
Whan I dinna ken whare I'm gaing,
Nor wha I hae to gae wi'?'

9.

9.[2] 'dey,' dairy-woman.

'My father, he is an auld shepherd,

My mither, she is an auld dey;
My name it is Donald Macdonald,
My name I'll never deny.'

10.
'O Donald, I'll gie ye five guineas
To sit ae hour in my room,
Till I tak aff your ruddy picture;
Whan I hae't, I'll never think lang.'
11.
'I dinna care for your five guineas;
It's ye that's the jewel to me;
I've plenty o' kye in the Hielands,
To feed ye wi' curds and green whey.
12.
'And ye'se get a bonnie blue plaidie,
Wi' red and green strips thro' it a';
And I'll be the lord o' your dwalling,
And that's the best picture ava'.
13.
'And I am laird o' a' my possessions;
The king canna boast o' na mair;
And ye'se hae my true heart in keeping,
There'll be na ither e'en hae a share.
14.
'Sae gae to the Hielands, my lassie,
O gae awa' happy wi' me;
O gae to the Hielands, Lizie Lindsay.
And hird the wee lammies wi' me.'

15.

'O how can I gae wi' a stranger,

Oure hills and oure glens frae my hame?'

'I tell ye I am Donald Macdonald;

I'll ever be proud o' my name.'

16.

Doun cam Lizie Lindsay's ain father,

A knicht o' a noble degree;

Says, 'If ye do steal my dear daughter,

It's hangit ye quickly sall be.'

17.

On his heel he turn'd round wi' a bouncie,

And a licht lauch he did gie;

'There's nae law in Edinbruch city

This day that can dare to hang me.'

18.

Then up bespak Lizie's best woman,

And a bonnie young lass was she;

'Had I but a mark in my pouchie,

It's Donald that I wad gae wi'.'

19.

19.[3] 'bare-hough'd,' with bare thighs.

'O Helen, wad ye leave your coffer,

And a' your silk kirtles sae braw,

And gang wi' a bare-hough'd puir laddie,

And leave father, mither, and a'?

20.

20.[1] 'warlock,' wizard.

'But I think he's a witch or a warlock,
Or something o' that fell degree,
For I'll gae awa' wi' young Donald,
Whatever my fortune may be.'

21.

Then Lizie laid doun her silk mantle,
And put on her waiting-maid's goun,
And aff and awa' to the Hielands
She's gane wi' this young shepherd loun.

22.

Thro' glens and oure mountains they wander'd,
Till Lizie had scantlie a shoe;
'Alas and ohone!' says fair Lizie,
'Sad was the first day I saw you!
I wish I war in Edinbruch city;
Fu' sair, sair this pastime I rue.'

23.

23.² 'shieling,' hut.

'O haud your tongue now, bonnie Lizie,
For yonder's the shieling, my hame,
And there's my guid auld honest mither,
That's coming to meet ye her lane.'

24.

'O ye're welcome, ye're welcome, Sir Donald,
Ye're welcome hame to your ain.'
'O ca' me na young Sir Donald,
But ca' me Donald my son.'
And this they hae spoken in Erse,

That Lizie micht not understand.

25.

25.[1] 'daggie,' drizzling.

The day being weetie and daggie,
They lay till 'twas lang o' the day.
'Win up, win up, bonnie Lizie,
And help at the milking the kye.'

26.

O slowly raise up Lizie Lindsay,
The saut tear blindit her e'e.
'O war I in Edinbruch city,
The Hielands shoud never see me!'

27.

He led her up to a hie mountain,
And bade her look out far and wide.
'I'm lord o' thae isles and thae mountains,
And ye're now my beautiful bride.

28.

'Sae rue na ye've come to the Hielands,
Sae rue na ye've come aff wi' me,
For ye're great Macdonald's braw lady,
And will be to the day that ye dee.'

THE GARDENER

THE TEXT of this pretty little song is taken from Kinloch's MSS., where it is in James Beattie's handwriting. In *Five Excellent New Songs*, printed at Edinburgh in 1766, there is an older but much corrupted version of this song, confused with two other songs, a 'Thyme' song and the favourite 'I sowed the seeds of love.' It is printed as two songs, *The New Lover's Garland* and *The Young Maid's Answer*, both with the following refrain:—

'Brave sailing here, my dear,

And better sailing there,

And brave sailing in my love's arms,

O if I were there!'

THE STORY is so slight that the song can scarcely be counted as a narrative. But it is one of the lyrical dialogues covered by the word 'ballad,' and was not ruled out by Professor Child. There seems to be a loss of half a verse in 7, which should doubtless be two stanzas.

THE GARDENER

1.

THE gardener stands in his bower-door,

With a primrose in his hand,

And by there came a leal maiden,

As jimp's a willow wand.

And by, etc.

2.

2.[4] 'weed,' dress.

'O lady, can you fancy me,

For to be my bride?

You'll get a' the flowers in my garden

To be to you a weed.

3.

'The lily white shall be your smock,

Becomes your body neat;

And your head shall be deck'd with jelly-flower,

And the primrose in your breast.

4.

4.² 'camovine,' camomile.

'Your gown shall be o' the sweet-william,

Your coat o' camovine,

And your apron o' the salads neat,

That taste baith sweet and fine.

5.

5.³ 'coot,' ankle.

5.⁴ 'brawn,' calf.

'Your stockings shall be o' the broad kail-blade,

That is baith broad and long;

And narrow, narrow at the coot,

And broad, broad at the brawn.

6.

'Your gloves shall be the marygold,

All glittering to your hand,

Well spread o'er wi' the blue blaewort,

That grows in corn-land.'

7.

'O fare you well, young man,' she says,

'Farewell, and I bid adieu;

Since you've provided a weed for me,

Among the summer flowers,

Then I'll provide another for you,

Among the winter showers.

8.

'The new-fallen snow to be your smock,

Becomes your body neat;

And your head shall be deck'd with the eastern wind,

And the cold rain on your breast.'

JOHN O' THE SIDE

> 'He is weil kend, Johne of the Syde,
>
> A greater theif did never ryde.'

SIR RICHARD MAITLAND.

THE TEXT is from the Percy Folio, but is given in modernised spelling. It lacks the beginning, probably, and one line in st. 3, which can be easily guessed; but as a whole it is an infinitely fresher and better ballad than that inserted in the *Minstrelsy* of Sir Walter Scott.

THE STORY is akin to that of *Kinmont Willie* (p. 49). John of the Side (on the river Liddel, nearly opposite Mangerton) first appears about 1550 in a list of freebooters against whom complaints were laid before the Bishop of Carlisle. He was, it seems, another of the Armstrong family.

Hobby Noble has a ballad5 to himself (as the hero of the present ballad deserves), in which mention is made of Peter of Whitfield. This is doubtless the person mentioned in the first line of *John o' the Side* as having been killed presumably by John himself.

'Culertun,' 10.1, is Chollerton on the Tyne. Percy suggests Challerton, and in the ballads upon which Scott founded his version the name is 'Cholerford.' 'Howbrame wood' and 'Lord Clough' are not identified; and Flanders files, effective as they appear to be, are not otherwise known.

'The ballad,' says Professor Child, 'is one of the best in the world, and enough to make a horse-trooper of any young borderer, had he lacked the impulse.'

5. Child, No. 189, from Caw's *Poetical Museum*, but not of sufficient merit to be included here.

JOHN O' THE SIDE

1.

PETER o' Whifield he hath slain,

And John o' Side, he is ta'en,

And John is bound both hand and foot,

And to the New-castle he is gone.

2.

But tidings came to the Sybil o' the Side,
By the water-side as she ran;
She took her kirtle by the hem,
And fast she run to Mangerton.
3.

   .   .   .   .   .

The lord was set down at his meat;
When these tidings she did him tell,
Never a morsel might he eat.
4.
But lords they wrung their fingers white,
Ladies did pull themselves by the hair,
Crying 'Alas and welladay!
For John o' the Side we shall never see more.
5.
'But we'll go sell our droves of kine,
And after them our oxen sell,
And after them our troops of sheep,
But we will loose him out of the New Castell.'

6.
But then bespake him Hobby Noble,
And spoke these words wondrous high;
Says, 'Give me five men to myself,
And I'll fetch John o' the Side to thee.'
7.
'Yea, thou'st have five, Hobby Noble,
Of the best that are in this country;
I'll give thee five thousand, Hobby Noble,

That walk in Tyvidale truly.'

8.

8.⁴ 'badgers,' corn-dealers or pedlars.

'Nay, I'll have but five,' says Hobby Noble,

'That shall walk away with me;

We will ride like no men of war,

But like poor badgers we will be.'

9.

9.² 'barefoot,' unshod.

They stuffed up all their bags with straw,

And their steeds barefoot must be;

'Come on, my brethren,' says Hobby Noble,

'Come on your ways, and go with me.'

10.

And when they came to Culerton ford,

The water was up, they could it not go;

And then they were ware of a good old man,

How his boy and he were at the plough.

11.

11.⁴ 'gate,' way.

'But stand you still,' says Hobby Noble,

'Stand you still here at this shore,

And I will ride to yonder old man,

And see where the gate it lies o'er.

12.

12.² 'see,' protect.

'But Christ you save, father!' quoth he,

'Christ both you save and see!

Where is the way over this ford?

For Christ's sake tell it me.'

13.

13.⁴ 'tree,' wood. The Folio gives '3'; Percy suggested the emendation.

'But I have dwelled here three score year,

So have I done three score and three;

I never saw man nor horse go o'er,

Except it were a horse of tree.'

14.

'But fare thou well, thou good old man!

The devil in hell I leave with thee,

No better comfort here this night

Thou gives my brethren here and me.'

15.

But when he came to his brether again,

And told this tidings full of woe,

And then they found a well good gate

They might ride o'er by two and two.

16.

And when they were come over the ford,

All safe gotten at the last,

'Thanks be to God!' says Hobby Noble,

'The worst of our peril is past.'

17.

And then they came into Howbrame wood,

And there then they found a tree,

And cut it down then by the root.

The length was thirty foot and three.

18.

And four of them did take the plank,

As light as it had been a flea,

And carried it to the New Castle,

Where as John o' Side did lie.

19.

And some did climb up by the walls,

And some did climb up by the tree,

Until they came up to the top of the castle,

Where John made his moan truly.

20.

He said, 'God be with thee, Sybil o' the Side!

My own mother thou art,' quoth he;

'If thou knew this night I were here,

A woe woman then wouldst thou be.

21.

'And fare you well, Lord Mangerton!

And ever I say God be with thee!

For if you knew this night I were here,

You would sell your land for to loose me.

22.

'And fare thou well, Much, Miller's son!

Much, Miller's son, I say;

Thou has been better at mirk midnight

Than ever thou was at noon o' the day.

23.

23.[3] 'him' = man, which is suggested by Furnivall.

'And fare thou well, my good lord Clough!

Thou art thy father's son and heir;

Thou never saw him in all thy life
But with him durst thou break a spear.

24.
'We are brothers childer nine or ten,
And sisters children ten or eleven;
We never came to the field to fight,
But the worst of us was counted a man.'
25.
But then bespake him Hobby Noble,
And spake these words unto him;
Says 'Sleepest thou, wakest thou, John o' the Side,
Or art thou this castle within?'
26.
'But who is there,' quoth John o' the Side,
'That knows my name so right and free?'
'I am a bastard-brother of thine;
This night I am comen for to loose thee.'
27.
'Now nay, now nay,' quoth John o' the Side,
'It fears me sore that will not be,
For a peck of gold and silver,' John said,
'In faith this night will not loose me.'
28.
28.4 'tent,' guard.
But then bespake him Hobby Noble,
And till his brother thus said he;
Says 'Four shall take this matter in hand,
And two shall tent our geldings free.'

29.
Four did break one door without,
Then John brake five himsel';
But when they came to the iron door,
It smote twelve upon the bell.

30.
'It fears me sore,' said Much, the Miller,
'That here taken we all shall be;'
'But go away, brethren,' said John o' the Side,
'For ever alas! this will not be.'
31.
'But fie upon thee!' said Hobby Noble;
'Much, the Miller, fie upon thee!
It sore fears me,' said Hobby Noble,
'Man that thou wilt never be.'
32.
But then he had Flanders files two or thee,
And he filed down that iron door,
And took John out of the New Castle,
And said 'Look thou never come here more!'
33.
When he had him forth of the New Castle,
'Away with me, John, thou shalt ride.'
But ever alas! it could not be,
For John could neither sit nor stride.
34.
But then he had sheets two or three,
And bound John's bolts fast to his feet,

And set him on a well good steed,

Himself on another by him set.

35.

35.¹ 'lough,' laughed.

Then Hobby Noble smiled and lough,

And spoke these words in mickle pride;

'Thou sits so finely on thy gelding

That, John, thou rides like a bride.'

36.

And when they came thorough Howbrame town,

John's horse there stumbled at a stone;

'Out and alas!' cried Much, the Miller,

'John, thou'll make us all be ta'en.'

37.

'But fie upon thee!' says Hobby Noble,

'Much, the Miller, fie on thee!

I know full well,' says Hobby Noble,

'Man that thou wilt never be.'

38.

And when they came into Howbrame wood,

He had Flanders files two or three

To file John's bolts beside his feet,

That he might ride more easily.

39.

39.² 'lope,' leapt.

Says 'John, now leap over a steed!'

And John then he lope over five.

'I know well,' says Hobby Noble,

'John, thy fellow is not alive.'

40.

Then he brought him home to Mangerton;

The lord then he was at his meat;

But when John o' the Side he there did see,

For fain he could no more eat.

41.

He says 'Blest be thou, Hobby Noble,

That ever thou wast man born!

Thou hast fetched us home good John o' the Side,

That was now clean from us gone.'

JAMIE DOUGLAS
AND
WALY, WALY, GIN LOVE BE BONNY

THE TEXT of the ballad is here given from Kinloch's MSS., where it is in the handwriting of John Hill Burton when a youth. The text of the song *Waly, waly*, I take from Ramsay's *Tea-Table Miscellany*. The song and the ballad have become inextricably confused, and the many variants of the former contain a greater or a smaller proportion of verses apparently taken from the latter.

THE STORY of the ballad as here told is nevertheless quite simple and straightforward. It is spoken in the first person by the daughter of the Earl of Mar. (She also says she is sister to the Duke of York, 7.[4], a person often introduced into ballads.) Blacklaywood, the lady complains, has spoken calumniously of her to her lord, and she leaves him, saying farewell to her children, and taking her youngest son with her.

The ballad is historical in so far as that Lady Barbara Erskine, daughter of the Earl of Mar, was married in 1670 to James, second Marquis of Douglas, and was formally separated from him in 1681. Further, tradition puts the blame of the separation on William Lawrie, factor to the Marquis, often styled the laird of Blackwood ('Blacklaywood,' 2.[3]), from his wife's family estate.

The non-historical points in the ballad are minor ones. The couple had only one child; and the lady's father could not have come to fetch her away (9.[2]), as the Earl of Mar died in 1668, before his daughter's wedding.

I have printed the song *Waly, waly* not because it can be considered a ballad, but simply because it is so closely interwoven with *Jamie Douglas*. Stanza 6 is reminiscent of the beautiful English quatrain beginning:

'Westron wind, when will thou blow.'

See Chappell's *Popular Music of the Olden Time*, i. 57.

JAMIE DOUGLAS

    1.

    1.[1] 'Waly' = alas!

    1.[4] 'wunt' = were wont.

    WALY, waly up the bank,

And waly, waly down the brae!

And waly, waly to yon burn-side,

Where me and my love wunt to gae!

2.

As I lay sick, and very sick,

And sick was I, and like to die,

And Blacklaywood put in my love's ears

That he staid in bower too lang wi' me.

3.

3.[4] 'lichtlie,' make light of.

As I lay sick, and very sick,

And sick was I, and like to die,

And walking into my garden green,

I heard my good lord lichtlie me.

4.

Now woe betide ye, Blacklaywood!

I'm sure an ill death you must die;

Ye'll part me and my ain good lord,

And his face again I'll never see.

5.

'Come down stairs now, Jamie Douglas,

Come down stairs and drink wine wi' me;

I'll set thee into a chair of gold,

And not one farthing shall it cost thee.'

6.

6.[3] 'baas,' balls.

'When cockle-shells turn silver bells,

And muscles grow on every tree,

When frost and snow turn fiery baas,
I'll come down the stair and drink wine wi' thee.'
7.
'What's needs me value you, Jamie Douglas,
More than you do value me?
The Earl of Mar is my father,
The Duke of York is my brother gay.
8.
'But when my father gets word o' this,
I trow a sorry man he'll be;
He'll send four score o' his soldiers brave,
To tak me hame to mine ain countrie.'
9.
As I lay owre my castell-wa',
I beheld my father comin' for me,
Wi' trumpets sounding on every side;
But they werena music at a' for me.

10.
'And fare ye weel now, Jamie Douglas!
And fare ye weel, my children three!
And fare ye weel, my own good lord!
For my face again ye shall never see.
11.
'And fare ye weel now, Jamie Douglas!
And fare ye weel, my children three!
And fare ye weel now, Jamie Douglas,
But my youngest son shall gae wi' me.'
12.

'What ails ye at your youngest son,
Sits smilin' at the nurse's knee?
I'm sure he never knew any harm,
Except it was from his nurse or thee.'
13.

. . . . .
. . . . .

And when I was into my coaches set,
He made his trumpets a' to soun.'
14.
I've heard it said, and it's oft times seen,
The hawk that flies far frae her nest;
And a' the world shall plainly see
It's Jamie Douglas that I love best.
15.
I've heard it said, and it's oft times seen,
The hawk that flies from tree to tree;
And a' the world shall plainly see
It's for Jamie Douglas I maun die.

WALY, WALY, GIN LOVE BE BONNY

1.
O WALY, waly up the bank!
And waly, waly, down the brae!
And waly, waly yon burn-side,
Where I and my love wont to gae!
2.
I lean'd my back unto an aik,
I thought it was a trusty tree;

But first it bow'd, and syne it brak,
Sae my true-love did lightly me.

3.

O waly, waly! but love be bonny
A little time, while it is new;
But when it is auld, it waxeth cauld,
And fades away like morning dew.

4.

O wherefore shoud I busk my head?
Or wherefore shoud I kame my hair?
For my true-love has me forsook,
And says he'll never love me mair.

5.

Now Arthur-Seat shall be my bed,
The sheets shall ne'er be fyl'd by me;
Saint Anton's well shall be my drink,
Since my true-love has forsaken me.

6.

Martinmas wind, when wilt thou blaw,
And shake the green leaves off the tree?
O gentle death, when wilt thou come?
For of my life I am weary.

7.

'Tis not the frost that freezes fell,
Nor blawing snaw's inclemency;
'Tis not sic cauld that makes me cry,
But my love's heart grown cauld to me.

8.

When we came in by Glasgow town,
We were a comely sight to see;
My love was cled in the black velvet,
And I mysell in cramasie.

9.

But had I wist, before I kiss'd,
That love had been sae ill to win,
I'd lock'd my heart in a case of gold,
And pin'd it with a silver pin.

10.

Oh, oh, if my young babe were born,
And set upon the nurse's knee,
And I mysell were dead and gane!
For a maid again I'll never be.

THE HEIR OF LINNE

THE TEXT is taken from the Percy Folio, but I have modernised the spelling. For the *Reliques* Percy made a ballad out of the Folio version combined with 'a modern ballad on a similar subject,' a broadside entitled *The Drunkard's Legacy*, thus producing a very good result which is about thrice the length of the Folio version.

The Scottish variant was noted by Motherwell and Buchan, but previous editors—Herd, Ritson, Chambers, Aytoun—had used Percy's composition.

THE STORY.—There are several Oriental stories which resemble the ballad as compounded by Percy from *The Drunkard's Legacy*. In most of these—Tartar, Turkish, Arabic, Persian, etc.—the climax of the story lies in the fact that the hero in attempting to hang himself by a rope fastened to the ceiling pulls down a hidden treasure. There is, of course, no such episode in *The Heir of Linne*, but all the stories have similar circumstances, and the majority present the moral aspect of unthriftiness, and of friends deserting a man who loses his wealth.

'Linne,' of course, is the place which is so often mentioned in ballads. See note, First Series, p. 1.

THE HEIR OF LINNE

1.

OF all the lords in fair Scotland

A song I will begin;

Amongst them all there dwelled a lord,

Which was the unthrifty lord of Linne.

2.

2.[3,4] Interchanged in manuscript.

2.[4] 'blin,' stop.

His father and mother were dead him fro,

And so was the head of all his kin;

To the cards and dice that he did run

He did neither cease nor blin.

3.

To drink the wine that was so clear,

With every man he would make merry;

And then bespake him John of the Scales,

Unto the heir of Linne said he;

4.

Says 'How dost thou, lord of Linne?

Dost either want gold or fee?

Wilt thou not sell thy lands so broad

To such a good fellow as me?

5.

5.¹ Deficient in manuscript.

5.⁴ 'God's penny,' an earnest-penny, to clinch a bargain.

'For   .   .   .   I
  .   .   .   ,' he said,

'My land, take it unto thee.'

'I draw you to record, my lordës all.'

With that he cast him a God's penny.

6.

He told him the gold upon the board,

It wanted never a bare penny.

'That gold is thine, the land is mine;

The heir of Linne I will be.'

7.

'Here's gold enough,' saith the heir of Linne,

'Both for me and my company.'

He drunk the wine that was so clear,

And with every man he made merry.

8.

Within three-quarters of a year
His gold and fee it waxed thin,
His merry men were from him gone,
And left him himself all alone.

9.

He had never a penny left in his purse,
Never a penny left but three,
And one was brass, and another was lead,
And another was white money.

10.

'Now welladay!' said the heir of Linne,
'Now welladay, and woe is me!
For when I was the lord of Linne,
I neither wanted gold nor fee.

11.

11.[3] 'read,' advice.

'For I have sold my lands so broad,
And have not left me one penny;
I must go now and take some read
Unto Edinburgh, and beg my bread.'

12.

He had not been in Edinburgh
Not three-quarters of a year,
But some did give him, and some said nay,
And some bid 'To the deil gang ye!

13.

13.[1] 'fere,' companion.

'For if we should hang any landless fere,

The first we would begin with thee.'

'Now welladay!' said the heir of Linne,

'Now welladay, and woe is me!

14.

14.² 'irk with,' weary of.

'For now I have sold my lands so broad,

That merry man is irk with me;

But when that I was the lord of Linne,

Then on my land I lived merrily.

15.

'And now I have sold my land so broad,

That I have not left me one penny!

God be with my father!' he said,

'On his land he lived merrily.'

16.

16.² 'unbethought him,' bethought himself. See *Old Robin of Portingale*, 5.³ (First Series, p. 14).

Still in a study there as he stood,

He unbethought him of a bill—

He unbethought him of a bill

Which his father had left with him.

17.

Bade him he should never on it look

Till he was in extreme need;

'And by my faith,' said the heir of Linne,

'Than now I had never more need.'

18.

18.⁴ 'in fere,' together.

He took the bill, and looked it on,

Good comfort that he found there;

It told him of a castle wall

Where there stood three chests in fere.

19.

19.[4] ? 'gold and fee.' Cp. 27.[4]

Two were full of the beaten gold,

The third was full of white money.

He turned then down his bags of bread,

And filled them full of gold so red.

20.

20.[4] Ritson said 'speer' was a hole in the wall of a house, through which the family received and answered the inquiries of strangers. This is apparently a mere conjecture.

Then he did never cease nor blin,

Till John of the Scales' house he did win.

When that he came to John of the Scales,

Up at the speer he looked then.

21.

There sat three lords upon a row,

And John o' the Scales sat at the board's head,

And John o' the Scales sat at the board's head,

Because he was the lord of Linne.

22.

22.[3] 'shot,' reckoning. Cp. 'pay the shot.'

And then bespake the heir of Linne,

To John o' the Scales' wife thus said he;

Said, 'Dame, wilt thou not trust me one shot

That I may sit down in this company?'

23.

'Now Christ's curse on my head,' she said,

'If I do trust thee one penny!'

Then bespake a good fellow,

Which sat by John o' the Scales his knee;

24.

Said, 'Have thou here, thou heir of Linne,

Forty pence I will lend thee;

Some time a good fellow thou hast been;

And other forty if need be.'

25.

They drunken wine that was so clear,

And every man they made merry;

And then bespake him John o' the Scales,

Unto the lord of Linne said he;

26.

Said, 'How dost thou, heir of Linne,

Since I did buy thy lands of thee?

I will sell it to thee twenty pound better cheap

Nor ever I did buy it of thee.'

27.

27.4 See 19.4 and note.

'I draw you to record, lordës all;'

With that he cast him a God's penny;

Then he took to his bags of bread,

And they were full of the gold so red.

28.

He told him the gold then over the board,

It wanted never a broad penny.

'That gold is thine, the land is mine,

And heir of Linne again I will be.'

29.

'Now welladay!' said John o' the Scales' wife,

'Welladay, and woe is me!

Yesterday I was the lady of Linne,

And now I am but John o' the Scales' wife!'

30.

Says 'Have thou here, thou good fellow,

Forty pence thou did lend me,

Forty pence thou did lend me,

And forty pound I will give thee.

31.

'I'll make thee keeper of my forest,

Both of the wild deer and the tame,'

.   .   .   .   .
.   .   .   .   .

32.

But then bespake the heir of Linne,

These were the words, and thus said he,

'Christ's curse light upon my crown,

If e'er my land stand in any jeopardy!'

EARL BOTHWELL

THE TEXT is from the Percy Folio, the spelling being modernised. Percy printed it (with alterations) in the *Reliques*.

THE STORY of the ballad represents that Darnley was murdered by way of revenge for his participation in the murder of Riccio; that Mary sent for Darnley to come to Scotland, and that she was finally banished by the Regent. All of these statements, and several minor ones, contain as much truth as may be expected in a ballad of this kind.

Mary escaped from Lochleven Castle on May 2, 1568, and found refuge in England on the 16th. The ballad was doubtless written shortly afterwards. On March 24, 1579, a 'ballad concerninge the murder of the late Kinge of Scottes' was licensed to Thomas Gosson, a well-known printer of broadsides.

EARL BOTHWELL

1.

1.[2] 'sleight,' trick.

WOE worth thee, woe worth thee, false Scotland!

For thou hast ever wrought by a sleight;

For the worthiest prince that ever was born

You hanged under a cloud by night.

2.

The Queen of France a letter wrote,

And sealed it with heart and ring,

And bade him come Scotland within,

And she would marry him and crown him king.

3.

3.[3,4] A popular proverb; see *The Lord of Learne*, 39.[3,4] (Second Series, p. 190).

To be a king, it is a pleasant thing,

To be a prince unto a peer;

But you have heard, and so have I too,

A man may well buy gold too dear.

4.

There was an Italian in that place

Was as well beloved as ever was he;

Lord David was his name,

Chamberlain unto the queen was he.

5.

For if the king had risen forth of his place,

He would have sit him down in the chair,

And tho' it beseemed him not so well,

Altho' the king had been present there.

6.

Some lords in Scotland waxed wonderous worth,

And quarrell'd with him for the nonce;

I shall you tell how it befell;

Twelve daggers were in him all at once.

7.

When this queen see the chamberlain was slain,

For him her cheeks she did weet,

And made a vow for a twelvemonth and a day

The king and she would not come in one sheet.

8.

Then some of the lords of Scotland waxed wroth,

And made their vow vehemently;

'For death of the queen's chamberlain

The king himself he shall die.'

9.

They strowed his chamber over with gun powder,
And laid green rushes in his way;
For the traitors thought that night
The worthy king for to betray.

10.

10.[1] 'made him boun,' prepared himself.
To bed the worthy king made him boun;
To take his rest, that was his desire;
He was no sooner cast on sleep
But his chamber was on a blazing fire.

11.

Up he lope, and a glass window broke,
He had thirty foot for to fall;
Lord Bodwell kept a privy watch
Underneath his castle wall.
'Who have we here?' said Lord Bodwell;
'Answer me, now I do call.'

12.

'King Henry the Eighth my uncle was;
Some pity show for his sweet sake!
Ah, Lord Bodwell, I know thee well;
Some pity on me I pray thee take!'

13.

'I'll pity thee as much,' he said,
'And as much favour I'll show to thee,
As thou had on the queen's chamberlain
That day thou deemedst him to die.'

14.

Through halls and towers this king they led,
Through castles and towers that were high,
Through an arbour into an orchard,
And there hanged him in a pear tree.

15.

When the governor of Scotland he heard tell
That the worthy king he was slain,
He hath banished the queen so bitterly
That in Scotland she dare not remain.

16.

But she is fled into merry England,
And Scotland too aside hath lain,
And through the Queen of England's good grace
Now in England she doth remain.

DURHAM FIELD

THE TEXT is another of the lively battle-pieces from the Percy Folio, put into modern spelling, and no other version is known or needed. The battle of Durham, which the minstrel says (27.[1], 64.[2]) was fought on a morning of May, and (64.[3,4]) within a month of Crecy and Poictiers,[6] actually took place on October 17, 1346. Stanza 18 makes the king say to Lord Hamilton that they are of 'kin full nigh'; and this provides an upper limit for the date of the ballad, as James Hamilton was married to Princess Mary, sister of James III., in 1474.

THE STORY.—We have as authorities for the history of the battle both Scottish and English chronicles, but the ballad, as might be expected, follows neither very closely. Indeed it is not easy to reconcile the Scottish account with the English. David Bruce, the young king of Scotland, seized the opportunity afforded by Edward III.'s absence in France at the siege of Calais to invade England with a large army. They were met at Durham by an English force in three divisions, led (according to the English chronicle) by (i) the Earl of Angus, Henry Percy, Ralph Neville, and Henry Scrope, (ii) the Archbishop of York, and (iii) Mowbray, Rokeby, and John of Copland. The Scots were also in three divisions, which were led (says the Scottish version) by King David, the Earl of Murray and William Douglas, and the Steward of Scotland and the Earl of March respectively. The English chronicle puts John of Douglas with the Earl of Murray, and the Earl of Buchan with King David.

The ballad, therefore, that calls Angus 'Anguish' (11.[1]) and puts him on the side of the Scots, as well as Neville (17.[1]), and apparently confuses the two Douglases (14 and 21), is not more at variance with history than is to be expected, and in the present case is but little more vague than the historical records themselves.

'Vaughan' (13.[1]) may be Baughan or Buchan, though it is doubtful whether there was an Earl of Buchan in 1346. 'Fluwilliams' (41.[3]) is perhaps a form of Llewellyn (Shakespeare spells it Fluellen), but this does not help to identify that lord.

<u>6.</u> Creçy was fought on August 26, 1346; Poictiers on September 19, 1356.

DURHAM FIELD

    1.

    1.[2] '[spell]' suggested by Child.

LORDINGS, listen and hold you still;

Hearken to me a little [spell];

I shall you tell of the fairest battle

That ever in England befell.

2.

For as it befell in Edward the Third's days,

In England, where he ware the crown,

Then all the chief chivalry of England

They busked and made them boun.

3.

They chosen all the best archers

That in England might be found,

And all was to fight with the King of France,

Within a little stound.

4.

And when our king was over the water,

And on the salt sea gone,

Then tidings into Scotland came

That all England was gone.

5.

Bows and arrows they were all forth,

At home was not left a man

But shepherds and millers both,

And priests with shaven crowns.

6.

6.³ 'leeve,' pleasant, dear; formerly a regular epithet of London.

Then the King of Scots in a study stood,

As he was a man of great might;

- 188 -

He sware he would hold his Parliament in leeve London,
If he could ride there right.

7.
Then bespake a squire, of Scotland born,
And said, 'My liege, apace,
Before you come to leeve London,
Full sore you'll rue that race.

8.
'There been bold yeomen in merry England,
Husbandmen stiff and strong;
Sharp swords they done wear,
Bearen bows and arrows long.'

9.
The King was angry at that word;
A long sword out he drew,
And there before his royal company
His own squire he slew.

10.
10.[1] 'Hard hansel,' bad omen.
Hard hansel had the Scots that day,
That wrought them woe enough,
For then durst not a Scot speak a word
For hanging at a bough.

11.
'The Earl of Anguish, where art thou?
In my coat-armour thou shalt be,
And thou shalt lead the forward
Thorough the English country.

12.

12.² 'stead,' place.

'Take thee York,' then said the King,
'In stead whereas it doth stand;
I'll make thy eldest son after thee
Heir of all Northumberland.

13.

'The Earl of Vaughan, where be ye?
In my coat-armour thou shalt be;
The high Peak and Derbyshire
I give it thee to thy fee.'

14.

14.¹ 'famous' may be a scribe's error for 'James.'

14.³ 'vanward,' vanguard.

Then came in famous Douglas,
Says 'What shall my meed be?
And I'll lead the vanward, lord,
Thorough the English country.'

15.

15.² The manuscript gives 'Tuxburye, Killingworth.'

'Take thee Worcester,' said the King,
'Tewkesbury, Kenilworth, Burton upon Trent;
Do thou not say another day
But I have given thee lands and rent.

16.

'Sir Richard of Edinburgh, where are ye?
A wise man in this war!
I'll give thee Bristow and the shire

The time that we come there.

17.

'My lord Nevill, where been ye?
You must in these wars be;
I'll give thee Shrewsbury,' says the King,
'And Coventry fair and free.

18.

'My lord of Hamilton, where art thou?
Thou art of my kin full nigh;
I'll give thee Lincoln and Lincolnshire,
And that's enough for thee.'

19.

19.² 'breme,' fierce.

By then came in William Douglas,
As breme as any boar;
He kneeled him down upon his knees,
In his heart he sighed sore.

20.

Says 'I have served you, my lovely liege,
These thirty winters and four,
And in the Marches between England and Scotland,
I have been wounded and beaten sore.

21.

'For all the good service that I have done,
What shall my meed be?
And I will lead the vanward
Thorough the English country.'

22.

'Ask on, Douglas,' said the King,

'And granted it shall be.'

'Why then, I ask little London,' says Will Douglas,

'Gotten if that it be.'

23.

The King was wrath, and rose away;

Says 'Nay, that cannot be!

For that I will keep for my chief chamber,

Gotten if it be.

24.

'But take thee North Wales and Westchester,

The country all round about,

And rewarded thou shalt be,

Of that take thou no doubt.'

25.

Five score knights he made on a day,

And dubb'd them with his hands;

Rewarded them right worthily

With the towns in merry England.

26.

26.[2] 'they busk them boun,' they make themselves ready.

And when the fresh knights they were made,

To battle they busk them boun;

James Douglas went before,

And he thought to have won him shoon.

27.

But they were met in a morning of May

With the communalty of little England;

But there scaped never a man away,

Through the might of Christës hand.

28.

But all only James Douglas;

In Durham in the field

An arrow struck him in the thigh;

Fast flings he towards the King.

29.

The King looked toward little Durham,

Says 'All things is not well!

For James Douglas bears an arrow in his thigh,

The head of it is of steel.

30.

'How now, James?' then said the King,

'How now, how may this be?

And where been all thy merry men

That thou took hence with thee?'

31.

31.⁴ 'gate,' way.

'But cease, my King,' says James Douglas,

'Alive is not left a man!'

'Now by my faith,' says the King of the Scots,

'That gate was evil gone.

32.

'But I'll revenge thy quarrel well,

And of that thou may be fain;

For one Scot will beat five Englishmen,

If they meeten them on the plain,'

33.

33.[4] 'tho,' then.

'Now hold your tongue,' says James Douglas,
'For in faith that is not so;
For one Englishman is worth five Scots,
When they meeten together tho.

34.
'For they are as eager men to fight
As a falcon upon a prey;
Alas! if ever they win the vanward,
There scapes no man away.'
35.
'O peace thy talking,' said the King,
'They be but English knaves,
But shepherds and millers both,
And priests with their staves.'
36.
The King sent forth one of his heralds of armes
To view the Englishmen.
'Be of good cheer,' the herald said,
'For against one we be ten.'
37.
'Who leads those lads,' said the King of Scots,
'Thou herald, tell thou me.'
The herald said 'The Bishop of Durham
Is captain of that company.
38.
'For the Bishop hath spread the King's banner,
And to battle he busks him boun.'

'I swear by St. Andrew's bones,' says the King,
'I'll rap that priest on the crown.'
39.
The King looked towards little Durham,
And that he well beheld,
That the Earl Percy was well armed,
With his battle-axe entered the field.

40.
40.² 'ancients,' ensigns.
The King looked again towards little Durham,
Four ancients there see he;
There were two standards, six in a valley,
He could not see them with his eye.
41.
My lord of York was one of them,
My lord of Carlisle was the other,
And my lord Fluwilliams,
The one came with the other.
42.
The Bishop of Durham commanded his men,
And shortly he them bade,
That never a man should go to the field to fight
Till he had served his God.
43.
Five hundred priests said mass that day
In Durham in the field,
And afterwards, as I heard say,
They bare both spear and shield.

44.

44.1 'orders,' prepares.

The Bishop of Durham orders himself to fight

With his battle-axe in his hand;

He said 'This day now I will fight

As long as I can stand!'

45.

45.4 'may,' = maid; the Virgin.

'And so will I,' said my lord of Carlisle,

'In this fair morning gay.'

'And so will I,' said my lord Fluwilliams,

'For Mary, that mild may.'

46.

46.4 'scantly,' scarcely.

Our English archers bent their bows

Shortly and anon;

They shot over the Scottish host

And scantly touched a man.

47.

'Hold down your hands,' said the Bishop of Durham,

'My archers good and true.'

The second shoot that they shot,

Full sore the Scots it rue.

48.

48.4 'cheer,' face, appearance.

The Bishop of Durham spoke on high

That both parties might hear,

'Be of good cheer, my merrymen all,

The Scots flien and changen their cheer.'

49.

49.⁴ 'dree,' hold out.

But as they saiden, so they diden,
They fell on heapës high;
Our Englishmen laid on with their bows
As fast as they might dree.

50.

The King of Scots in a study stood
Amongst his company;
An arrow struck him thorough the nose,
And thorough his armoury.

51.

The King went to a marsh-side
And light beside his steed;
He leaned him down on his sword-hilts
To let his nose bleed.

52.

There followed him a yeoman of merry England,
His name was John of Copland;
'Yield thee, traitor!' says Copland then,
'Thy life lies in my hand.'

53.

53.² 'And,' if.

'How should I yield me,' says the King,
'And thou art no gentleman?'
'No, by my troth,' says Copland there,
'I am but a poor yeoman.

54.
'What art thou better than I, sir King?
Tell me, if that thou can!
What art thou better than I, sir King,
Now we be but man to man?'

55.
The King smote angrily at Copland then,
Angrily in that stound;
And then Copland was a bold yeoman,
And bore the King to the ground.

56.
He set the King upon a palfrey,
Himself upon a steed;
He took him by the bridle-rein,
Towards London he gan him lead.

57.
And when to London that he came,
The King from France was new come home,
And there unto the King of Scots
He said these words anon.

58.
'How like you my shepherds and my millers?
My priests with shaven crowns?'
'By my faith, they are the sorest fighting men
That ever I met on the ground.

59.
'There was never a yeoman in merry England
But he was worth a Scottish knight.'

'Ay, by my troth,' said King Edward, and laugh,

'For you fought all against the right.'

60.

But now the prince of merry England

Worthily under his shield

Hath taken the King of France,

At Poictiers in the field.

61.

61.[1] 'food,' man.

The prince did present his father with that food,

The lovely King of France,

And forward of his journey he is gone.

God send us all good chance!

62.

62.[1] The last five words are perhaps inserted by the scribe.

62.[3] 'leve,' grant.

'You are welcome, brother!' said the King of Scots to the King of France,

'For I am come hither too soon;

Christ leve that I had taken my way

Unto the court of Rome!'

63.

'And so would I,' said the King of France,

'When I came over the stream,

That I had taken my journey

Unto Jerusalem!'

64.

Thus ends the battle of fair Durham,

In one morning of May,

The battle of Creçy, and the battle of Poictiers,

All within one monthës day.

65.

Then was wealth and welfare in merry England,

Solaces, game, and glee,

And every man loved other well,

And the king loved good yeomanry.

66.

But God that made the grass to grow,

And leaves on greenwood tree,

Now save and keep our noble King,

And maintain good yeomanry!

THE BATTLE OF HARLAW

THE TEXT of this ballad was sent to Professor Child by Mr. C. E. Dalrymple of Kinaldie, Aberdeenshire, from whose version the printed variants (*Notes and Queries*, Third Series, vii. 393, and Aytoun's *Ballads of Scotland*, i. 75) have been more or less directly derived.

The ballad is one of those mentioned in *The Complaynt of Scotland* (1549), like the 'Hunttis of Chevet' (see p. 2 of this volume). It is again mentioned as being in print in 1668; but the latter may possibly refer to a poem on the battle, afterwards printed in Allan Ramsay's *Evergreen*. The fact that the present ballad omits all reference to the Earl of Mar, and deals with the Forbes brothers, who are not otherwise known to have taken part in the battle, disposes Professor Child to believe that it is a comparatively recent ballad.

THE STORY.—The battle of Harlaw was fought on July 24, 1411. Harlaw is eighteen miles north-west of Aberdeen, Dunidier a hill on the Aberdeen road, and Netherha' is close at hand. Balquhain (2.²) is a mile south of Harlaw, while Drumminnor (15.³) is more than twenty miles away—though the horse covered the distance there and back in 'twa hours an' a quarter' (16.³).

The ballad is narrated by 'John Hielan'man' to Sir James the Rose (derived from the ballad of that name given earlier in the present volume) and Sir John the Gryme (Graeme). 'Macdonell' is Donald of the Isles, who, as claimant to the Earldom of Ross, advanced on Aberdeen, and was met at Harlaw by the Earl of Mar and Alexander Ogilvy, sheriff of Angus. It was a stubborn fight, though it did not last from Monday to Saturday (23), and Donald lost nine hundred men and the other party five hundred.

Child finds a difficulty with the use of the word 'she' in 4.³, despite 'me' in the two previous lines. Had it been 'her,' the difficulty would not have arisen.

THE BATTLE OF HARLAW

1.

AS I cam in by Dunidier,

An' doun by Netherha',

There was fifty thousand Hielan'men

A-marching to Harlaw.

Wi' a dree dree dradie drumtie dree

2.

As I cam on, an' farther on,
An' doun an' by Balquhain,
Oh there I met Sir James the Rose,
Wi' him Sir John the Gryme.

3.

'O cam ye frae the Hielan's, man?
An' cam ye a' the wey?
Saw ye Macdonell an' his men,
As they cam frae the Skee?'

4.

'Yes, me cam frae ta Hielan's, man,
An' me cam a' ta wey,
An' she saw Macdonell an' his men,
As they cam frae ta Skee.'

5.

'Oh was ye near Macdonell's men?
Did ye their numbers see?
Come, tell to me, John Hielan'man,
What micht their numbers be?'

6.

'Yes, me was near, an' near eneuch,
An' me their numbers saw;
There was fifty thousan' Hielan'men
A-marchin' to Harlaw.'

7.

'Gin that be true,' says James the Rose,

'We'll no come meikle speed;
We'll cry upo' our merry men,
And lichtly mount our steed.'

8.
'Oh no, oh no,' says John the Gryme,
'That thing maun never be;
The gallant Grymes were never bate,
We'll try phat we can dee.'

9.
As I cam on, an' farther on,
An' doun an' by Harlaw,
They fell fu' close on ilka side;
Sic fun ye never saw.

10.
They fell fu' close on ilka side,
Sic fun ye never saw;
For Hielan' swords gied clash for clash
At the battle o' Harlaw.

11.
The Hielan'men, wi' their lang swords,
They laid on us fu' sair,
An' they drave back our merry men
Three acres breadth an' mair.

12.
Brave Forbës to his brither did say,
'Noo, brither, dinna ye see?
They beat us back on ilka side,
An' we'se be forced to flee.'

13.

'Oh no, oh no, my brither dear,

That thing maun never be;

Tak' ye your good sword in your hand,

An' come your wa's wi' me.'

14.

'Oh no, oh no, my brither dear,

The clans they are ower strang,

An' they drive back our merry men,

Wi' swords baith sharp an' lang.'

15.

15.[4] 'fess,' fetch.

Brave Forbës drew his men aside,

Said 'Tak' your rest awhile,

Until I to Drumminnor send,

To fess my coat o' mail.'

16.

The servant he did ride,

An' his horse it did na fail,

For in twa hours an' a quarter

He brocht the coat o' mail.

17.

Then back to back the brithers twa

Gaed in amo' the thrang,

An' they hewed doun the Hielan'men,

Wi' swords baith sharp an' lang.

18.

Macdonell he was young an' stout,

Had on his coat o' mail,

An' he has gane oot throw them a',

To try his han' himsell.

19.

19.[1] 'ae,' one.

The first ae straik that Forbës strack,

He garrt Macdonell reel,

An' the neist ae straik that Forbës strack,

The great Macdonell fell.

20.

20.[1] 'lierachie,' confusion, hubbub.

An' siccan a lierachie

I'm sure ye never saw

As wis amo' the Hielan'men,

When they saw Macdonell fa'.

21.

An' whan they saw that he was deid,

They turn'd an' ran awa,

An' they buried him in Leggett's Den,

A large mile frae Harlaw.

22.

They rade, they ran, an' some did gang,

They were o' sma' record;

But Forbës an' his merry men,

They slew them a' the road.

23.

On Monanday, at mornin',

The battle it began,

On Saturday, at gloamin',

Ye'd scarce kent wha had wan.

24.
An' sic a weary buryin'
I'm sure ye never saw
As wis the Sunday after that,
On the muirs aneath Harlaw.
25.
25.[1] 'speer at,' ask of.
Gin ony body speer at you
For them ye took awa',
Ye may tell their wives and bairnies
They're sleepin' at Harlaw.

THE LAIRD OF KNOTTINGTON

THE TEXT was sent to Percy in 1768 by R. Lambe of Norham. The ballad is widely known in Scotland under several titles, but the most usual is *The Broom of Cowdenknows*, which was the title used by Scott in the *Minstrelsy*.

THE STORY is not consistently told in this version, as in 11.[3,4] the daughter gives away her secret to her father in an absurd fashion.

An English song, printed as a broadside about 1640, *The Lovely Northerne Lasse*, is directed to be sung 'to a pleasant Scotch tune, called The broom of Cowden Knowes.' It is a poor variant of our ballad, in the usual broadside style, and cannot have been written by any one fully acquainted with the Scottish ballad. It is in the Roxburghe, Douce, and other collections.

THE LAIRD OF KNOTTINGTON

1.

1.[2] 'knows,' knolls.

1.[4] 'bught,' sheep-pen.

THERE was a troop of merry gentlemen

Was riding atween twa knows,

And they heard the voice of a bonny lass,

In a bught milking her ews.

2.

There's ane o' them lighted frae off his steed,

And has ty'd him to a tree,

And he's gane away to yon ew-bught,

To hear what it might be.

3.

'O pity me, fair maid,' he said,

'Take pity upon me;

O pity me, and my milk-white steed

That's trembling at yon tree.'

4.

'As for your steed, he shall not want

The best of corn and hay;

But as to you yoursel', kind sir,

I've naething for to say.'

5.

He's taen her by the milk-white hand,

And by the green gown-sleeve,

And he has led her into the ew-bught,

Of her friends he speer'd nae leave.

6.

He has put his hand in his pocket,

And given her guineas three;

'If I dinna come back in half a year,

Then luke nae mair for me.

7.

'Now show to me the king's hie street,

Now show to me the way;

Now show to me the king's hie street,

And the fair water of Tay.'

8.

She show'd to him the king's hie street,

She show'd to him the way;

She show'd him the way that he was to go,

By the fair water of Tay.

9.

9.[4] 'your lain,' by yourself.

When she came hame, her father said,

'Come, tell to me right plain;

I doubt you've met some in the way,

You have not been your lain.'

10.

'The night it is baith mist and mirk,

You may gan out and see;

The night is mirk and misty too,

There's nae body been wi' me.

11.

11.[1] 'tod,' fox.

'There was a tod came to your flock,

The like I ne'er did see;

When he spake, he lifted his hat,

He had a bonny twinkling ee.'

12.

When fifteen weeks were past and gane,

Full fifteen weeks and three,

Then she began to think it lang

For the man wi' the twinkling ee.

13.

It fell out on a certain day,

When she cawd out her father's ky,

There was a troop of gentlemen

Came merrily riding by.

14.

'Weel may ye sigh and sob,' says ane,

'Weel may you sigh and see;

Weel may you sigh and say, fair maid,

Wha's gotten this bairn wi' thee?'

15.

She turned hersel' then quickly about,

And thinking meikle shame;

'O no, kind sir, it is na sae,

For it has a dad at hame.'

16.

'O hawd your tongue, my bonny lass,

Sae loud as I hear you lee!

For dinna you mind that summer night

I was in the bught wi' thee?'

17.

He lighted off his milk-white steed,

And set this fair maid on;

'Now caw out your ky, good father,' he said,

'She'll ne'er caw them out again.

18.

18.² 'plows': as much land as a plough will till in a year.

'I am the laird of Knottington,

I've fifty plows and three;

I've gotten now the bonniest lass

That is in the hale country.'

THE WHUMMIL BORE

THE TEXT is from Motherwell's MS. He included it in the Appendix to his *Minstrelsy*. No other collector or editor notices the ballad—'if it ever were one,' as Child remarks.

The only point to be noted is that the second stanza has crept into two versions of *Hind Horn*, apparently because of the resemblance of the previous stanzas, which present a mere ballad-commonplace.

THE WHUMMIL BORE

1.

1.[2,4,5] The burden is of course repeated in each stanza.

SEVEN lang years I hae served the king,

Fa fa fa fa lilly

And I never got a sight of his daughter but ane.

With my glimpy, glimpy, glimpy eedle,

Lillum too tee a ta too a tee a ta a tally

2.

2.[1] 'whummil bore,' a hole bored with a whimble or gimlet.

I saw her thro' a whummil bore,

And I ne'er got a sight of her no more.

3.

Twa was putting on her gown,

And ten was putting pins therein.

4.

Twa was putting on her shoon,

And twa was buckling them again.

5.
Five was combing down her hair,
And I never got a sight of her nae mair.
6.
Her neck and breast was like the snow,
Then from the bore I was forced to go.

LORD MAXWELL'S LAST GOODNIGHT

THE TEXT is from the Glenriddell MSS., and is the one on which Sir Walter Scott based the version given in the *Border Minstrelsy*. Byron notes in the preface to *Childe Harold* that 'the good-night in the beginning of the first canto was suggested by Lord Maxwell's Goodnight in the Border Minstrelsy.'

THE STORY.—John, ninth Lord Maxwell, killed Sir James Johnstone in 1608; the feud between the families was of long standing (see 3.[4]), beginning in 1585. Lord Maxwell fled the country, and was sentenced to death in his absence. On his return in 1612 he was betrayed by a kinsman, and beheaded at Edinburgh on May 21, 1613. This was the end of the feud, which contained cases of treachery and perfidy on both sides.

'Robert of Oarchyardtoun' was Sir Robert Maxwell of Orchardton, Lord Maxwell's cousin.

'Drumlanrig,' 'Cloesburn,' and 'the laird of Lagg' were respectively named Douglas, Kirkpatrick, and Grierson.

The Maxwells had houses, or custody of houses at Dumfries, Lochmaben, Langholm, and Thrieve; and Carlaverock Castle is still theirs.

As for Lord Maxwell's 'lady and only joy,' the ballad neglects the fact that he instituted a process of divorce against her, and that she died, while it was pending, in 1608, five years before the date of the 'Goodnight.'

LORD MAXWELL'S LAST GOODNIGHT

1.

'ADIEW, madam my mother dear,

But and my sisters two!

Adiew, fair Robert of Oarchyardtoun

For thee my heart is woe.

2.

'Adiew, the lilly and the rose,

The primrose, sweet to see!

Adiew, my lady and only joy!

For I manna stay with thee.

3.

3.² 'feed,' feud.

3.⁴ 'dead,' death.

'Tho' I have killed the laird Johnston,

What care I for his feed?

My noble mind dis still incline;

He was my father's dead.

4.

'Both night and day I laboured oft

Of him revenged to be,

And now I've got what I long sought;

But I manna stay with thee.

5.

'Adiew, Drumlanrig! false was ay,

And Cloesburn! in a band,

Where the laird of Lagg fra my father fled

When the Johnston struck off his hand.

6.

'They were three brethren in a band;

Joy may they never see!

But now I've got what I long sought,

And I maunna stay with thee.

7.

'Adiew, Dumfries, my proper place,

But and Carlaverock fair!

Adiew, the castle of the Thrieve,

And all my buildings there!

8.

8.² 'shank,' point of a hill.

'Adiew, Lochmaben's gates so fair,
The Langholm shank, where birks they be!
Adiew, my lady and only joy!
And, trust me, I maunna stay with thee.

9.

9.³ 'bangisters,' roisterers, freebooters.

'Adiew, fair Eskdale, up and down,
Where my poor friends do dwell!
The bangisters will ding them down,
And will them sore compel.

10.

'But I'll revenge that feed mysell
When I come ou'r the sea;
Adiew, my lady and only joy!
For I maunna stay with thee.'

11.

'Lord of the land, will you go then
Unto my father's place,
And walk into their gardens green,
And I will you embrace.

12.

'Ten thousand times I'll kiss your face,
And sport, and make you merry.'
'I thank thee, my lady, for thy kindness,
But, trust me, I maunna stay with thee.'

13.

Then he took off a great gold ring,

Whereat hang signets three;

'Hae, take thee that, my ain dear thing,

And still hae mind of me;

14.

14.[1] 'But if,' unless.

'But if thow marry another lord

Ere I come ou'r the sea;

Adiew, my lady and only joy!

For I maunna stay with thee.'

15.

The wind was fair, the ship was close,

That good lord went away,

And most part of his friends were there,

To give him a fair convay.

16.

They drank thair wine, they did not spare,

Even in the good lord's sight;

Now he is o'er the floods so gray,

And Lord Maxwell has ta'en his goodnight.

END OF THE THIRD SERIES

APPENDIX

THE JOLLY JUGGLER

THE TEXT is from a manuscript at Balliol College, Oxford, No. 354, already referred to in the First Series (p. 80) as supplying a text of *The Nut-brown Maid*. The manuscript, which is of the early part of the sixteenth century, has been edited by Ewald Flügel in *Anglia*, vol. xxvi., where the present ballad appears on pp. 278-9. I have only modernised the spelling, and broken up the lines, as the ballad is written in two long lines and a short one to each stanza.

No other text is known to me. The volume of *Anglia* containing the ballad was not published till 1903, some five years after Professor Child's death; and I believe he would have included it in his collection had he known of it.

THE STORY narrates the subjugation of a proud lady who scorns all her wooers, by a juggler who assumes the guise of a knight. On the morrow the lady discovers her paramour to be a churl, and he is led away to execution, but escapes by juggling himself into a meal-bag: the dust falls in the lady's eye.

It would doubtless require a skilled folk-lorist to supply full critical notes and parallels; but I subjoin such details as I have been able to collect.

In *The Beggar Laddie* (Child, No. 280, v. 116) a pretended beggar or shepherd-boy induces a lassie to follow him, 'because he was a bonny laddie.' They come to his father's (or brother's) hall; he knocks, four-and-twenty gentlemen welcome him in, and as many gay ladies attend the lassie, who is thenceforward a knight's or squire's lady.

In *The Jolly Beggar* (Child, No. 279, v. 109), which, with the similar Scottish poem *The Gaberlunzie Man*, is attributed without authority to James V. of Scotland, a beggar takes up his quarters in a house, and will only lie behind the hall-door, or by the fire. The lassie rises to bar the door, and is seized by the beggar. He asks if there are dogs in the town, as they would steal all his 'meal-pocks.' She throws the meal-pocks over the wall, saying, 'The deil go with your meal-pocks, my maidenhead, and a'.' The beggar reveals himself as a braw gentleman.

A converse story is afforded by the first part of the Norse tale translated by Dasent in *Popular Tales from the Norse*, 1888, p. 39, under the title of *Hacon Grizzlebeard*. A princess refuses all suitors, and mocks them publicly. Hacon Grizzlebeard, a prince, comes to woo her. She makes the king's fool mutilate the prince's horses, and then makes game of his appearance as he drives out the next day. Resolved to take his revenge, Hacon disguises himself as a beggar, attracts the princess's notice by means of a golden spinning-wheel, its stand, and a golden wool-winder, and sells them to her for the privilege of sleeping firstly outside her door, secondly beside her bed, and finally in it. The rest of the tale narrates Hacon's method of breaking down the princess's pride.

Other parallels of incident and phraseology may be noted:—

4.[1] 'well good steed'; 'well good,' a commonplace = very good; for 'well good steed,' cf. *John o' the Side*, 34.[3] (p. 162 of this volume).

7.[1] 'Four-and-twenty knights.' The number is a commonplace in ballads; especially cf. *The Beggar Laddie* (as above), Child's text A, st. 13:

> 'Four an' tuenty gentelmen
>
> They conved the beager ben,
>
> An' as mony gay ladës
>
> Conved the beager's lassie.'

12.[4] For the proper mediæval horror of 'churl's blood,' see *Glasgerion*, stt. 12, 19 (First Series, pp. 4, 5).

13.[3] 'meal-pock.' The meal-bag was part of the professional beggar's outfit; see *Will Stewart and John*, 78.[3] (Child, No. 107, ii. 437). For blinding with meal-dust, see *Robin Hood and the Beggar*, ii. 77, 78 (Child, No. 134, iii. 163). The meal-pock also occurs in *The Jolly Beggar*, as cited above.

THE JOLLY JUGGLER

> Draw me near, draw me near,
>
> Draw me near, ye jolly jugglere!

1.

> HERE beside dwelleth
>
> A rich baron's daughter;
>
> She would have no man
>
> That for her love had sought her.
>
> *So nice she was!*

2.

2.[3] 'But if,' unless.

> She would have no man

That was made of mould,

But if he had a mouth of gold

To kiss her when she would.

So dangerous she was!

3.

3.⁴ 'teen,' wrath.

Thereof heard a jolly juggler

That laid was on the green;

And at this lady's words

I wis he had great teen.

An-ang'red he was!

4.

He juggled to him a well good steed

Of an old horse-bone,

A saddle and a bridle both,

And set himself thereon.

A juggler he was!

5.

5.³, 6.³ 'wend,' thought.

5.³ 'had' omitted in the manuscript.

He pricked and pranced both

Before that lady's gate;

She wend he [had] been an angel

Was come for her sake.

A pricker he was!

6.

He pricked and pranced

Before that lady's bower;

She wend he had been an angel

Come from heaven tower.

A prancer he was!

7.

Four-and-twenty knights

Led him into the hall,

And as many squires

His horse to the stall,

And gave him meat.

8.

8.³ 'He': the manuscript reads '&.'

They gave him oats

And also hay;

He was an old shrew

And held his head away.

He would not eat.

9.

The day began to pass,

The night began to come,

To bed was brought

The fair gentlewoman,

And the juggler also.

10.

The night began to pass,

The day began to spring;

All the birds of her bower,

They began to sing,

And the cuckoo also!

11.

'Where be ye, my merry maidens,

That ye come not me to?

The jolly windows of my bower

Look that you undo,

That I may see!

12.

'For I have in mine arms

A duke or else an earl.'

But when she looked him upon,

He was a blear-eyed churl.

'Alas!' she said.

13.

13.³ 'meal-pock,' meal-bag.

She led him to an hill,

And hanged should he be.

He juggled himself to a meal-pock;

The dust fell in her eye;

Beguiled she was.

14.

14.³ 'giglot,' wench.

God and our Lady

And sweet Saint Joham

Send every giglot of this town

Such another leman,

Even as he was!

www.ingramcontent.com/pod-product-compliance
Ingram Content Group UK Ltd.
Pitfield, Milton Keynes, MK11 3LW, UK
UKHW040816280325
456847UK00003B/466